TOM LYCOS: Born in Aberystwyth, Wales, of Greek and English parents, Tom spent two years working with renowned Dutch company KISS before returning to Australia to join Sidetrack Theatre as an ensemble member in 1985. In 1988, he played the lead male role in Jane Campion's film *Sweetie*. He was then acrobat/musician/performer with Circus Oz for three years and then actor/musician in two stage musicals, *Buddy* and *Escape from the Forbidden Planet*. He has performed with Melbourne Theatre Company, Arena Theatre, Griffin Theatre, Melbourne Workers Theatre, Back to Back Theatre and Kinetic Energy. In 1994, he was co-deviser/actor in the Burning House production of *That Eye the Sky* with Hugo Weaving and David Wenham, directed by Richard Roxburgh. In 1996, Tom joined Zeal Theatre, co-creating eight original productions with co-collaborator Stefo Nantsou, including *The Stones*, *Burnt* and *Taboo* (which Tom has also directed for TheatreHaus in Frankfurt, Germany, and Teater Grimsborken in Oslo, Norway).

STEFO NANTSOU: Born in Newcastle, Australia, of Macedonian parents, Stefo has written, co-created, directed and acted in over 120 theatre productions for companies throughout Australia, Europe, North America, Asia, South Africa and New Zealand in his 30-year career. After co-founding the Ship-O-Fools in 1980, and working as an ensemble actor/writer with Sidetrack Theatre and Freewheels Theatre, he founded Zeal Theatre in 1989. Zeal has created over 40 original productions including *The Stones*, which has been performed over 1,100 times worldwide including seasons at the National Theatre in London and The Duke Theatre in New York, and translated and performed in over 25 countries worldwide. Stefo has also directed his plays for companies in Germany, Holland, Wales, Hungary, Canada and Denmark. He is currently the resident director at the Sydney Theatre Company, still writing and performing new works with Zeal Theatre, and is guest 'regie' with Australian Macedonian Theatre in Sydney.

Founded in 1989 by actor/writer/director Stefo Nantsou, Zeal Theatre is a touring theatre company which has created over 40 original productions, including works for theatres, schools, outdoor site-specific events and festivals, family shows and a range of international co-productions. Zeal's 'house' style incorporates live music with a range of theatrical styles and a bare-bones, no-frills aesthetic focusing on the skills of the performer. Zeal's work is known worldwide, the company having performed throughout Europe, North America, Asia, South Africa and New Zealand, with many of Zeal's plays now being translated and produced in many countries; including *The Stones*, *Australia v South Africa* and *Taboo* by Tom Lycos and Stefo Nantsou, and *The Apology* and *The Forwards* by Stefo Nantsou. Zeal Theatre received the prestigious ASSITEJ International President's Award for 'excellence in the profession of theatre' in Montreal, Canada in 2005.

the ZEAL theatre collection

Tom Lycos and Stefo Nantsou

THE STONES / BURNT / TABOO

CURRENCY PRESS
SYDNEY

CURRENCY PLAYS

First published in 2011
by Currency Press Pty Ltd,
PO Box 2287, Strawberry Hills, NSW, 2012, Australia
enquiries@currency.com.au
www.currency.com.au

NATIONAL LIBRARY OF AUSTRALIA CIP DATA

Author:	Nantsou, Stefo.
Title:	The Zeal Theatre collection / Stefo Nantsou and Tom Lycos.
ISBN:	9780868199061 (pbk.)
Subjects:	Australian drama–21st century.
Other Authors / Contributors:	
	Lycos, Tom. Zeal Theatre.
Dewey Number:	A822.3

Foreword

The work of Zeal has been a vital and steadily increasing part of the identity of Sydney Theatre Company (STC) for ten years or so. Initially it was a kind of umbrella connection, made through *The Stones*, which was an extant show toured into schools all over Sydney and NSW. Commissions followed, with work in schools for the education arm of the company becoming a regular and on-going collaboration between STC and Zeal. This connection became ever-broader with the *Burnt* project as the work reached beyond schools and into communities (specifically rural communities suffering under the burden of drought). For a small company, Zeal Theatre has a massive reach, a broad appeal and a phenomenal output.

The scripts in this book are indicators of that output, but indicators only because every Zeal show is different—and we mean every performance of every Zeal show. This is because more than anything else Zeal is alive. The work is highly theatrical in the time-honoured tradition of travelling players (vagabonds, blackguards and rogues they are)—from Commedia dell'Arte through to AGITPROP—Zeal are keepers of a flame where theatre is connected directly to its audience, fuelled by their concerns and their questions, charged with their well-being and the quandaries that endanger their very hearts and souls on a daily basis. In lesser hands, it would be synopsised and marginalised as 'issue-based with educational outcomes', but Zeal is so, so, so much more than that. They are aware of the traditions that their work springs from and aware of the terrible greyness that separates the black from the white in every vexing issue that we face. That we face when we are thirteen, sixteen, thirty-six and sixty-four. That we should face with a shudder and/or a laugh. Zeal produces theatre through and through, 100-proof. Theatre guaranteed to make you so blind that you can truly see Oedipus.

Enjoy the read and remember if you set out to mount these shows yourself or plan on using them as a model for developing your own work: the script really is just the tip of a mighty theatrical iceberg.

Andrew Upton and Cate Blanchett

Andrew Upton and Cate Blanchett are Artistic Directors of the Sydney Theatre Company.

The book has been printed on paper certified by the
Programme for the Endorsement of Forest Certification
(PEFC). PEFC is committed to sustainable forest
management through third party forest certification of
responsibly managed forests.

PEFC/21-31-17

Australian Government

Australia | Council
for the Arts

Publication of this title was assisted by
the Commonwealth Government through
the Australia Council, its arts funding and
advisory body.

Typeset by Dean Nottle for Currency Press.
Printed by Ligare Pty Ltd, Riverwood, NSW.
Front cover shows Tom Lycos and Stefo Nantsou in a publicity image for *The Stones*. Photograph by Ponch Hawkes.

Contents

Stefo Nantsou as Yahoo (left) and Tom Lycos as Shy Boy in the Zeal Theatre production of THE STONES. *(Photo: Tracy Schramm)*

THE STONES

INTRODUCTION:
'FOR A STRICTLY LIMITED SEASON ONLY!'

We worked together for three years as part of the full-time performing ensemble at Sidetrack Theatre in Sydney 1985–87, developing a similar style and approach to our work. It seemed inevitable that, one day, we would make a two-hander for ourselves. After leaving Sidetrack, Tom played a lead role in Jane Campion's film *Sweetie*, had a few roles on TV, performed in two long-running stage musicals and was a long-time acrobat/musician with Circus Oz. Stefo founded Zeal Theatre in 1989 and was building the company's reputation around Australia and New Zealand, creating original productions for schools, theatres and festivals. By 1996, both of us were living in Melbourne. We hadn't seen each other for years, but when we finally caught up, within an hour we had decided to make that two-hander we'd said we'd make one day. Then we had a jam on our guitars and started talking about what it might be.

The Stones was inspired by a true story, where two teenage boys, aged thirteen and fifteen, were charged with manslaughter after kicking rocks off a freeway overpass and killing a motorist. We were interested in the question 'were these boys old enough to be responsible for their actions?', and we wanted to write a play which posed that question to audiences of the same age as the boys as well as to adults. We developed the script with the assistance of the police officer who was in charge of the real case. After that four-hour interview at Homicide Headquarters, we made all our artistic decisions about the script and the play in the elevator on our way down to the car. We'd play two kids and two cops; we'd wear tracksuits with zipper up for kids and zipper down revealing a shirt and tie for the cops; we'd start the play with the boys running amok, the death of the motorist would be about halfway through and we'd end with the verdict.

We also researched other similar incidents from around the world. We were not interested in creating a 'documentary-style' drama of the 'true' events of one real story. We used the skeleton structure of the real case, fictionalising the characters as if they could be two boys, anywhere and at anytime. We created a narrative form, keeping focus on the boys and the two police officers who charge them and sit with them throughout their trial. We wrote the play in around two to three months, over a part-time period, and rehearsed for eight days before the first performance.

The Stones premiered in Melbourne in May 1996. On the original promotional poster is printed 'For a strictly limited season only!' We have since performed the play over 1,100 times worldwide, including seasons at the Royal National Theatre in London, the New Victory Theater in New York, De Krakling in Amsterdam and a cow shed in Zain-Horn on the Danube in Austria. The play has been translated and produced in over 25 countries. We have directed the play for other theatre companies in Germany, Canada, Wales, Holland, Hungary, Denmark and Norway.

The Stones has received numerous national and international awards, with Zeal Theatre being awarded the prestigious ASSITEJ International Directors' Choice Award for 'excellence in the theatre for young people industry' in Montreal, Canada in 2005.

Tom Lycos and Stefo Nantsou
December 2010

FIRST PRODUCTION

The Stones was first performed at Trinity College, Melbourne, on 13 June 1996 with the following cast:

SHY BOY / QUINN	Tom Lycos
YAHOO / RUSSO	Stefo Nantsou

Directed and designed by Tom Lycos and Stefo Nantsou

CHARACTERS

SHY BOY, 13-year-old schoolboy

YAHOO, 15-year-old boy

RUSSO, detective

QUINN, detective

Note: *The Stones* is a dramatised true story written as a play for two actors. The two actors play two roles each, moving from teenage character to detective character by the simple use of a zipper on a tracksuit; zipped fully up for the teenager, zipped down, revealing a white collar and tie, for the detective. The actors employ full use of verbal sound effects and miming objects throughout the performance, with the exception of torches, petrol can and lighter. The actors should also play the music live.

PROLOGUE

SHY BOY *stands on a freeway overpass looking down at the passing traffic. The wind howls quietly and he shivers from the cold.*

The wind picks up and SHY BOY *struggles against the blowing gale until he gives up and leaves the overpass. (*YAHOO *is making the wind sounds with his guitar.)*

SHY BOY *joins* YAHOO, *picking up a guitar and starting to play a riff as the scene shifts to Yahoo's lounge room.*

YAHOO *stops the wind sound and picks up the riff as if it is a game.*

They play an instrumental piece on their guitars, trying all the while to outdo each other with their guitar skills.

When the instrumental finishes they invite applause from the audience, put the guitars down and come forward to start the story.

SCENE ONE: BREAK AND ENTER

YAHOO *and* SHY BOY *are running as fast as they can. They jump a few fences and eventually reach the side of a large warehouse.*

SHY BOY: [*pointing towards a side door*] It's over there… cool.

> *They move over to the door.* YAHOO *tries opening it, but it's locked. He tries shaking it open, but the door makes too much noise. So he stops.*

It was open before.
YAHOO: Well, it's locked now.
SHY BOY: You probably locked it.
YAHOO: Oh, shut ya face.
SHY BOY: Give us a go.
YAHOO: Don't touch it.
SHY BOY: Why not?
YAHOO: You'll set off some sort of stupid alarm or something.
SHY BOY: I will not.
YAHOO: Yes you will.

> *They both laugh nervously.*

Hey look, you stay here, see if the security guy comes, and I'll go around the other side and see if we can get in there. Don't touch the door.

> YAHOO *moves around to the other side of the warehouse while* SHY BOY *stands at the locked door.* SHY BOY, *very impatient, decides he'll try kicking the door open.* YAHOO *hears the banging sound from the other side of the warehouse and creeps back over to* SHY BOY *and stops him kicking the door.*

Shut up, you dickhead. Why don't you go and call the cops, tell 'em what we're doin'?

SHY BOY: Sorry.

YAHOO: I said don't touch the door.

SHY BOY: I said sorry.

YAHOO: And I said don't touch the door.

> *They laugh nervously again.*

Come on, let's go around the other side.

SHY BOY: [*noticing a window*] Hey!

YAHOO: What?

SHY BOY: Check this out.

YAHOO: [*very interested*] Oh. Hey, get up there.

> YAHOO *gives* SHY BOY *a lift up to see through the window.* SHY BOY *looks in a little while, then jumps back down.*

SHY BOY: [*loudly*] There's a BMW!

YAHOO: [*covering* SHY BOY'*s mouth*] Keep ya voice down, okay!

SHY BOY: [*recovering quickly*] There's a BMW in there and it's got one of them badge things on it.

YAHOO: Great. Did ya open the window?

SHY BOY: Na.

YAHOO: Well, get up there and open the window, dickhead. Hurry up.

> YAHOO *lifts* SHY BOY *up again and he tries opening the window.*

SHY BOY: Stand still.

YAHOO: Shut ya face.

> SHY BOY *tries again, then jumps back down.* YAHOO *thinks he's succeeded.*

Excellent!

SHY BOY: It's locked.

YAHOO: Well, let's go around the other side.

SHY BOY: Okay.

> *They creep around to the other side of the warehouse, where* YAHOO *sees another window, this one higher than the other.*

YAHOO: Hey, get up there.

SHY BOY: Shhh.

YAHOO: Hurry up.

> SHY BOY *climbs up on* YAHOO*'s shoulders.*

I got ya… I won't wobble, hurry up… I got ya… I got ya—shit, I'm gonna drop ya…

> SHY BOY *almost falls, but successfully climbs up on* YAHOO*'s shoulders and looks through the window.*

SHY BOY: Hey!

YAHOO: What?

SHY BOY: There's a yellow ute.

YAHOO: Excellent.

SHY BOY: There's all this stuff in the back.

YAHOO: Okay, open the window.

SHY BOY: There's a window lock.

YAHOO: Well, unlock it.

SHY BOY: There's a window lock.

YAHOO: Unlock it.

SHY BOY: I told ya there's a win—

> YAHOO *angrily drops* SHY BOY *off his shoulders.*

YAHOO: I thought you wanted to break in.

SHY BOY: Yeah, I told ya—

YAHOO: That was your idea.

SHY BOY: Yeah, but if ya just listen—

YAHOO: You said let's go down the warehouse and break in.

SHY BOY: Yeah, but will you just let me say—

YAHOO: You can't even open a stupid window, can ya?!

SHY BOY: I'm tryin' to tell ya—

YAHOO: Why don't you go home!

SHY BOY: [*hurt*] Oh?

YAHOO: Go on, piss off. Useless prick.

Pause.

SHY BOY:Ya big turd.

YAHOO: You stupid idiot dickhead prick turd.

SHY BOY: Stuff you.

YAHOO: Oh, stuff you. Why don't you go home and watch 'Play School', ya little baby.

SHY BOY: Shut up.

YAHOO: Shut up yourself.

They start walking around the warehouse in opposite directions.

SHY BOY: Man, I told ya right from the start we probably couldn't get in, eh…

YAHOO: Shut ya face.

SHY BOY: … but you had to go and try it.

YAHOO: Piss off home.

SHY BOY: Stuff you.

YAHOO: Stuff you.

SHY BOY: Man, I knew it all along we couldn't get in.

YAHOO *sees a stormwater drain which leads under the warehouse.*

YAHOO: Hey! Come here.

SHY BOY *comes over sulkily.*

Check this out… Look, look. That's a stormwater drain (drain, drain, drain).

His voice echoes.

We can get in under there, man. Maybe there's a grill thing or something, we can get inside and open the door from the inside.

YAHOO/SHY BOY: Go on then!

YAHOO: No you go.

SHY BOY: No way.

YAHOO: Yeah, come on.

YAHOO *tries pulling* SHY BOY *towards the drain.*

SHY BOY: I'm not getting in there.

YAHOO: Yes you are.

SHY BOY: There's all rat turds and stuff.

YAHOO: Man, you're little, I'm big, I can't fit in there.

SHY BOY: No way.

YAHOO: [*storming off*] Okay! Forget it. I thought you wanted to break in.

SHY BOY: [*stopping him*] Alright, alright. I'll do it.

YAHOO: [*cheering up immediately*] Good on ya.

YAHOO *comes over and pushes* SHY BOY *towards the drain.*

SHY BOY: You don't have to push.

YAHOO: Get in.

SHY BOY: [*resisting*] I said I'll do it.

YAHOO: Get in!

YAHOO *pushes* SHY BOY *into a big pile of sewage in the drain.* SHY BOY *looks up at him disgusted at the revolting smell and mess.*

SHY BOY: Oh man.

YAHOO: Don't worry about the shit, just crawl in.

SHY BOY *crawls up the drain.* YAHOO *kneels down to look up the drain, and kneels in some shit.*

SHY BOY: Oh shit. It's disgusting (disgusting, disgusting, disgusting).

YAHOO: Shut ya face (shut ya face, shut ya face, shut ya face). Can you get in (get in, get in, get in)?

SHY BOY *has reached a grille and pushes it open and pops his head through the manhole.*

Are you in yet (are you in yet, are you in yet?)

SHY BOY: [*to himself*] Oh, man, this is sick as… check it out.

He crawls through the manhole into the warehouse and starts looking around. YAHOO *can't see a thing inside the drain.*

YAHOO: What are ya doin', man (man, man, man?)

SHY BOY: [*inside, to himself*] A BMW… cool.

SHY BOY *runs over to a corner in the warehouse and pisses along the wall and all over the back of the ute.*

YAHOO: [*angry and impatient*] Stop pissin' around and open the door, will ya (open the door will ya, will ya?)

SHY BOY *runs over to the door and swings it open, scaring* YAHOO. YAHOO *then gets inside too.*

SHY BOY: Man, I was already in through the thing…

YAHOO: Yeah, and I was outside screamin' and shoutin', ya dickhead.

> YAHOO *looks around quickly outside and shuts the door. The two look at each other in triumph.*

YAHOO/SHY BOY : Excellent!

SHY BOY: Check out this ute. There's all this stuff in the back.

> *They both look in the back of the ute. Then* YAHOO *notices the BMW.*

YAHOO: Oh… look at this BMW… it's brand new. Hey, it's got one of them badge things and everything. Matho reckons we can get fifty bucks for one of these down at the wreckers. Look for something to get it off.

> *Meanwhile* SHY BOY *has found a can of petrol in the back of the ute, unscrewed the lid, has crept over to* YAHOO *and starts splashing him with petrol.*

[*Shocked*] Hey… that's petrol, man… what are ya doin?!

SHY BOY: [*laughing*] I got you all down that side.

YAHOO: You think it's funny, eh?!

SHY BOY: You're soaked, look at that!

YAHOO: [*walking towards him*] You want to see something that's funny, do ya?

SHY BOY: [*still laughing*] Sucked in.

> YAHOO *pulls a lighter out of his pocket and lights it up and points it towards* SHY BOY. SHY BOY *stops laughing and backs away in horror.*

YAHOO: Where's ya petrol now, dickhead?!

> YAHOO, *satisfied with the threat, moves away.* SHY BOY *knows he's lucky he's not in flames.*

SHY BOY: That's stupid.

YAHOO: Why don't you pour petrol on yourself, go on, pour it all over yourself… and I'll burn ya balls off.

SHY BOY: You're crazy.

YAHOO: You're crazy, now put the petrol away, look for something to get this badge off.

> *He turns his attention back to the BMW.*

SHY BOY: Yeah.

YAHOO: And we can hurry up and go.

> *While* YAHOO *looks around for something to get the emblem off with,* SHY BOY *finds a large screwdriver in the back of the ute and holds it up in the air, ninja-style. He aims it at* YAHOO, *let's out some Chinese-like sounds and pretends to throw the screwdriver at* YAHOO. *He spins it through the air and straight into the back of* YAHOO *who immediately plays along, screaming in pain and agony. He struggles to get the screwdriver off* SHY BOY, *turns quickly and pretends to stab him in the stomach. Then he pretends to cut* SHY BOY'*s throat, then he pretends to cut his ear off and eat it.* SHY BOY *is in full gory blood-spilling action TV mode. He pretends there is blood pouring out of him. He holds his heart in his hand as if it is still beating.* YAHOO *realises the use of the screwdriver and goes back over to the BMW with it. He wants* SHY BOY'*s attention back.*

Hey, dickhead. Dickhead!

> SHY BOY *stops what he's doing and gives* YAHOO *his attention.*

SHY BOY: What?

YAHOO: Get off the floor, stop makin' so much noise, come over here and have a look at this.

> YAHOO *has got the screwdriver ready to get the emblem off the BMW.* SHY BOY *looks on nervously.*

SHY BOY: What are ya doin?

YAHOO: I'm getting the badge off. Hey, is there a badge on the boot? Go and see if there's a badge on the boot.

SHY BOY: [*whispering*] Yeah.

YAHOO: Excellent, I'm gonna get this badge off, and you're gonna get that badge off, so come over here and see how I'm gonna get this badge off.

SHY BOY: I can see. Hurry up.

YAHOO: Shhh.

SHY BOY: What if someone comes?

YAHOO: Shut up. We'll get these badges and we'll go. You see where I've got it?

SHY BOY: Yeah.
YAHOO: Fifty bucks each, man, easy money.

> *He hits the screwdriver onto the car and the car alarm goes off very loud. They stand in shock.*

Get ya can… get ya can… it's got your fingerprints on it… get the can, shut this door and crawl out through the shit.

> YAHOO *goes out the door,* SHY BOY *slams it shut, and heads down the drain.* YAHOO *waits outside as* SHY BOY *appears at the drain entrance without the can of petrol.*

Where's ya can? Go back and get the can. It's got your fingerprints all over it. Go back!

> SHY BOY *crawls quickly back through the drain, sticks his head back inside the warehouse, reaches for the can, and crawls back to the entrance of the drain with the can, the car alarm still blasting loudly.*

Run!

> *They run away from the warehouse, jumping back over a few fences on their way. They eventually stop running, look behind them and break into huge laughter and celebration.*

SHY BOY: That was close.

> YAHOO *drops the screwdriver and starts having a major asthma attack.* SHY BOY *doesn't notice, picks up the screwdriver and keeps playing.*

Hey, that's mine… Ha, cool.

> SHY BOY *then notices* YAHOO *sitting, gasping for breath.*

What's wrong? Come on, let's go… let's just go, eh?!
YAHOO: [*barely able to speak*] Wait a minute.
SHY BOY: Let's go.

> SHY BOY *runs off.* YAHOO *is left alone gasping for breath.*

SCENE TWO: WAREHOUSE INVESTIGATION

Two detectives, QUINN *and* RUSSO, *are at the warehouse in response to the car alarm. They investigate the area with torches.*

RUSSO: All the windows are still locked and bolted from the inside. There's no sign of forced entry anywhere. That door over there is locked and bolted too. Through here, there's an office... there's a fax machine, computer, safety deposit box, but nothing's been touched at all. Owner said the car alarm has never gone off before, he reckons it might've been a pussycat. What do you reckon?

QUINN: There are a lot of cats in the area.

RUSSO: So you agree with the owner?

QUINN: There's petrol been spilt from here to there. Something's attacked the BMW emblem with a screwdriver, and there's cat piss over here in the corner.

RUSSO: So, we got ourselves a computer-illiterate, petrol-sniffing, pyro-maniac kitten with a weak bladder.

QUINN: Two.

RUSSO: What do you mean two?

QUINN: With hands.

RUSSO: Oh right, two pissed cats with hands?!

QUINN: I powdered the ute, there's two sets of prints. Looks like they got out through this mouse hole, and they've taken the petrol with them.

RUSSO: Is that all you've got?

QUINN *produces a ventolin spray.*

QUINN: One of the cats has asthma.

RUSSO: Well, you better go tell the owner the good news.

QUINN: No, you go.

RUSSO: You're better at explaining the asthmatic kittens than I am.

QUINN: Oh, come on, Russo, I'm always tellin' the owner the good news.

RUSSO: And you are very good at it.

QUINN: Alright, I'll go.

RUSSO: Good. And bring the car around while you're at it.

QUINN: Yeah, right.

QUINN *leaves.* RUSSO *shines his torch around the warehouse.*

RUSSO: Here kitty, kitty...

SCENE THREE: RECKLESSLY ENDANGERING LIFE

The two boys are setting fire to bushes. Suddenly their firebugging is interrupted by the sound of a cat. They find the cat, catch it, pour petrol over it, go to set it on fire too, but it escapes. Someone comes out of their house across the road, and the boys run off. They stop to catch their breath.

SHY BOY: You wouldn't have done it.

YAHOO: Woulda.

SHY BOY: What if it'd run into that building all on fire, man, the whole place woulda burnt down.

YAHOO: Yeah… I woulda done it if it was a dog. They burn better.

They find themselves at a rock pool. There are stones all around.

SHY BOY: This is the creek where the Abos are building that rock thing.

YAHOO: You wanna go see if Matho's at the video shop. Wanna see if he's there?

SHY BOY *skims stones across the pool.* YAHOO *gets nervous and bored.*

SHY BOY: Pretty scary place.

YAHOO: [*sarcastic*] Yeah, I'm shittin' mi pants.

SHY BOY: It's all really sacred, I reckon.

YAHOO: Are you scared of some weird Abo joint or somethin', are ya?

SHY BOY: Mum reckons Aboriginals have sacred sites.

YAHOO: Your mum is so smart. Look out… dreamtime!

YAHOO *pushes* SHY BOY *into the water and laughs loudly. They begin throwing rocks at each other.* SHY BOY *picks up a big flat stone.*

SHY BOY: This one is like a UFO.

YAHOO: This one's a bomb.

YAHOO *drops his rock on* SHY BOY*'s rock, the water splashing all over them.*

SHY BOY: Yeah, let's make them bombs.

He starts collecting big stones. YAHOO *joins him.*

YAHOO: Yeah, we'll make them bombs, let's bomb the shit out of that frog.

SHY BOY: No… let's take them back to Matho's.

YAHOO: Yeah, we can bomb the shit out of his garage.

They gather a whole stack of stones from the riverbank then head off and come to an overpass bridge above the freeway. YAHOO *stops and looks down at the traffic.*

Man, look at this red Monaro. I'm gonna get one of them.

SHY BOY: I'm gonna get a Volvo.

YAHOO: They're a heap of shit.

SHY BOY: They're stronger than Monaros when you smash 'em.

YAHOO: Man, this is wicked.

SHY BOY: What?

YAHOO: This, up here.

SHY BOY: All the cars and that. Look at this truck. What a bomb.

YAHOO: Throw a rock on the roof, scare the shit outta the driver.

They watch as the truck passes under them.

Oh, man, why didn't you throw a rock on the roof and scare the shit out of the driver?

SHY BOY: You see if you can hit one. Bet ya can't.

YAHOO: I bet I can.

YAHOO *places his stones in a line across the edge of the overpass.*

SHY BOY: No, come on, ya gotta chuck 'em.

YAHOO: I'm gonna line mine up and kick 'em off. That way no-one'll see me chuck 'em. Hey, why don't you line yours up too? We'll have one big line of rocks and we'll take it turns to kick 'em off. Come on.

SHY BOY: Right-oh.

SHY BOY *follows* YAHOO's *example and lines up his stones accordingly.*

YAHOO: Okay, here comes a truck, you go first.

SHY BOY: No, you go first.

YAHOO: No… you gotta go first.

SHY BOY: I'm not goin' first, you go first.

The truck passes under them. YAHOO *loses his temper agian.*

YAHOO: Alright we won't play then, Christ, you're gutless. You said you were gonna play and now you won't do it, okay.

SHY BOY: Okay, okay, I'll chuck mine, I just wanna see you do it first.

YAHOO: You're so gutless. Okay, here's a truck in my lane, you watch this.

YAHOO *kicks his stone off and it misses the truck.*

YAHOO/SHY BOY: Missed it! Man…

YAHOO: Nearly got it.

SHY BOY: Crap, you missed by a mile.

YAHOO: I did not.

SHY BOY: Did so.

YAHOO: Okay, you see if you can hit the next truck.

SHY BOY: Right-oh.

> *They wait for another truck. It does not come. Impatience settles in.*

YAHOO: Man, now there's not gonna be another truck, see, that's all your fault.

SHY BOY: Wait forever for another truck. Let's go to Matho's…

YAHOO: [*excited*] Commodore! See if you can hit that Commodore, it's in your lane.

SHY BOY: Yeah, right-oh…

> SHY BOY *kicks the stone and it too misses the target.*

SHY BOY/YAHOO: Oooooo, that was close, man… unreal… hahaha…

YAHOO: Here's a Falcon in my lane, watch this.

> YAHOO *kicks a stone off and misses the Falcon.*

SHY BOY/YAHOO: Oooo, that was close.

SHY BOY: Hey, Toyota.

YAHOO: Let's do two at once.

SHY BOY: Right-oh.

> *They both kick rocks onto the Toyota.*

YAHOO/SHY BOY: [*imitating a car commercial*] 'Oh, what a feeling!'

SHY BOY: I got one rock left.

YAHOO: Here comes a Volvo, get one of your favourites… go on, go, go go!

SHY BOY: Right-oh.

> SHY BOY *kicks the last stone and it smashes through the windscreen of the passing Volvo. There is a momentary silence. Pause. The boys look at each other.*

Let's go.

YAHOO: Yeah.

> *They run off the bridge and back through the creek area, where they stop for a while.*

SHY BOY: Reckon anyone saw us?

YAHOO: Na.

SHY BOY: What if someone saw us?

YAHOO: No-one's around, it's Sunday.

SHY BOY: Man, did you see it go straight through the windscreen, it shattered everywhere.

YAHOO: Yeah… I gotta go home now. See you at school tomorrow.

SHY BOY: Okay.

YAHOO: Don't tell anyone, will ya?!

SHY BOY: As if.

YAHOO: I said don't tell anyone, okay?

SHY BOY: I won't.

YAHOO: Okay… See ya!

SHY BOY: Yeah, see ya.

> YAHOO *runs off.* SHY BOY *is left on his own.*

SCENE FOUR: OVERPASS INVESTIGATION

QUINN is at the freeway overpass site. He is looking up at the overpass bridge, and working out a few things in his mind. RUSSO enters.

RUSSO: Three or four other cars were hit. One passenger hit on the side of the head, lucky to be alive. The dead guy is a university lecturer. No-one answering at his home address, we can't find his wife anywhere.

QUINN: I don't know whether he died from the fallen rock or the impact into the other car.

RUSSO: Well, if some pissed bloke threw a rock from up there, at a car that's going a hundred ks, did you see the hole in the guy's chest?

QUINN: No, but Russo, he must've been still alive.

RUSSO: No way. There was nothing left of his heart or his lungs, he was dead.

QUINN: But he drove a kilomctre up the road.

RUSSO: The car's going a hundred ks, it's only gonna take a coupla seconds to go a kilometre…

QUINN: I'm going up on the bridge to take a look.

RUSSO: No, you gotta help me and Phil find the wife first.

QUINN: I just want to have another look on the bridge.

> QUINN *leaves.* RUSSO *stands looking up at where his partner is going.*

RUSSO: Oh come on, you won't see anything now, it's too dark. I'm gonna help Phil find the wife, okay?

> RUSSO *leaves too as music starts, the scene shifts.*

> *Yahoo's place.* YAHOO *rushes through the door and looks around.*

YAHOO: Mum? Mum?

> *There is no response. He runs to another part of the house.*

Mum?!

> *Nobody home. He looks around as fear wells up in his stomach. He runs off.*

SCENE FIVE: SURRENDER

SHY BOY *is running as fast as he can. After running for some time, he stops to catch his breath. He is in shock.*

SHY BOY: I felt real bad after we ran off home. I was scared shitless. I know I'd done something real bad. My mum had made dinner. She asked where I'd been. She asked me if I'd been chased by a doberman, that I looked pale as a ghost. She asked if I was feeling sick. I told her I just wanted to go to my room and lay down. I heard the news come on the tele, how the rock killed a guy on the freeway. I felt my heart going too fast. I went to the bathroom and dry retched and got real shaky 'cause I knew it was me. I went back to my room and lay down. My mum comes in and asks if I'm alright. I lied to her because I was so scared. I wanted to tell her the truth but I couldn't. I wanted to tell someone what I'd done. Why didn't the guy just see the rock and drive around it? He could've driven around it. They said on the tele he was dead.

I couldn't sleep. Kept looking at the clock. I thought I gotta go to sleep, and try and be normal. The next morning I was trying to be really normal. Mum said I could stay at home. I said I was feeling alright and I forced myself to eat breakfast, like a normal kid, and then go to school. Then I thought the police might be there waiting for me. Then my mum says you're all nervy this morning. I walked into the street with my bike. The neighbour said hello, she was always friendly and made me embarrassed. I rode my bike halfway to school and got off near the creek and couldn't help it, I cried a lot because I didn't know what to do. I knew I couldn't be normal anymore. I thought about running away. I was at that spot by the river a long time. I got on my bike. I went home and I told Mum, she looked at me, she didn't move much, she kept just looking and being real still, then she said, 'Get in the car, we're going to be brave and tell the police'. I wasn't going to cry now. I wanted to know what was going to happen to me. I never thought I'd ever kill anyone. I'm only thirteen.

SCENE SIX: MANSLAUGHTER

RUSSO *is in his office. He is very busy.* SHY BOY *is waiting at the door. For a long time* RUSSO *does not notice* SHY BOY*'s presence. Eventually he does.*

RUSSO: You right, mate?

> *No answer.*

You looking for someone?

> *Still no answer.*

Come in?

> SHY BOY *doesn't move.*

I said come in, mate, come on, get out of the doorway…

> RUSSO *calls to another detective.*

Hey Phil? Can you go ask Tracy at the front desk who sent me this work experience kid in. And how come I always get them? [*He returns his attention to* SHY BOY.] Sit down.

> RUSSO *returns to what he was doing. Pause.*

So you wanna be a police officer, do you? What school do you go to?

SHY BOY: I'm the one who threw the rock off the bridge that killed that guy.

RUSSO: Oh yeah. [*Pause. It dawns on him what the boy said.*] What did you say? Say that again, mate?

SHY BOY: I'm the one that killed the guy, with the rock off the bridge.

> RUSSO *leaves the room to get* QUINN. *The two detectives stand at the door looking and whispering about* SHY BOY. *They then enter for an interview.*

RUSSO: Okay, mate, my name is Detective Russo, this is Detective Quinn.

SHY BOY: [*refering to* QUINN] Does he have to come in…?

RUSSO: Don't worry about Detective Quinn, that's just the look on his face. Now we're going to ask you a few questions, you don't have to say or do anything if you don't want to, but I have to tell you that this interview is going to be recorded. Is that alright with you?

SHY BOY: Alright.

RUSSO: Now… tell me, in your own words, exactly what happened on the day.

> *The actor playing* SHY BOY *'becomes'* QUINN. YAHOO *is now being interviewed by* QUINN. *(The two interviews take place simultaneously, with the actors switching quickly from detective to kid.)*

QUINN: What were you doing yesterday afternoon around five thirty?

RUSSO: Were you on your own?

QUINN: Who else was with you at the time?

RUSSO: And what's his name?

QUINN: Where does he live?

RUSSO: Was he with you when it happened?

QUINN: Whose idea was it to throw the stones?

RUSSO: What were you trying to do?

QUINN: How many stones did you throw?

RUSSO: Were you aiming at the cars?

QUINN: How many cars did you hit?

RUSSO: How many cars did your mate hit?

QUINN: Who threw the last stone?

RUSSO: How old are you?

YAHOO: I'm fifteen.

QUINN: And how old is your mate?

YAHOO: He's thirteen.

QUINN: And where do you know him from?

YAHOO: From school.

QUINN: Was anyone else with you?

YAHOO: No.

QUINN: Just the two of you?

YAHOO: Yeah... we didn't mean to kill anyone, honest.

QUINN: You were just having fun?

YAHOO: Yeah... that's all we were doin'.

QUINN: How many rocks did you kick off the bridge?

YAHOO: A few.

QUINN: Did you kick any of the rocks?

YAHOO: Yeah.

QUINN: Did you kick the last rock?

YAHOO: No.

QUINN: Are you sure?

YAHOO: Yes.

QUINN: Are you sure?

YAHOO: Yes... Look, I've already answered this question a hundred times, why do you keep askin' me the same stupid questions for?

QUINN: We just need to know all the facts.

RUSSO: Tell me again what happened.

SHY BOY: I've told you already.

RUSSO: Tell me again.

SHY BOY: Where from?

RUSSO: From when you got to the rock pool.

SHY BOY: That's where we got the rocks.

RUSSO: How many did you get?

SHY BOY: I dunno...

RUSSO: Big ones, little ones?

SHY BOY: A whole stack of 'em...

RUSSO: Just the big ones?

SHY BOY: I dunno, some were bigger than others.

RUSSO: How many did you take up on the bridge?

SHY BOY: I dunno.

RUSSO: How many? Five?

SHY BOY: Yeah.

RUSSO: Ten?

SHY BOY: Maybe.

RUSSO: Twenty?

SHY BOY: I dunno.

RUSSO: Twenty-five?

SHY BOY: Maybe.

RUSSO: Come on, mate, how many rocks?

SHY BOY: I can't remember!

> *The two officers then read the boys their rights together, their vocals overlapping until they say 'Do you understand?' together.*

QUINN: You have the right to contact a friend or relative. You have the right to contact a legal practitioner. If you are not an Australian citizen you can contact the Consular Office of your own country. You are not obliged to say or do anything. You have the right to remain silent. I must tell you that anything you say will be recorded and may be used as evidence in a court of law. Do you understand?

RUSSO: I am charging you with manslaughter. I am also charging you with seven separate counts of conduct recklessly endangering life. You will be remanded in custody to appear in the Melbourne Children's Court tomorrow. Do you understand?

YAHOO/SHY BOY: Yeah.

> *Pause. The boys, now alone, look at each other, and giggle.*

YAHOO: We made the front page. 'Two teens face trial over freeway rock death'. 'Boy, thirteen, surrenders to police'! 'Boy, thirteen, admits rock hit car'!

SHY BOY: 'Boy, thirteen, haunted by rock death'!

SCENE SEVEN: THE LADDER

The boys are now in separate cells.

SHY BOY: [*narrating*] They kept us in gaol overnight. Man, I couldn't sleep. I just kept seeing it over and over in my head. Kept havin' this weird dream... couldn't sleep... kept seein' it over and over...

> *He begins to fall asleep. He wakes up suddenly and sees* YAHOO *standing behind a tall ladder suspended in air.*

Oh, man. That's sick. How'd you do that?

YAHOO: You reckon you can climb up to the top?

SHY BOY: Na.

YAHOO: Yes you can.

SHY BOY: I'll do it for ten bucks.

YAHOO: No, just see if you can climb it.

SHY BOY: I'll do it for five bucks.

YAHOO: Come on. Are you scared of a stupid ladder? You're not gonna fall. It's only a dream.

SHY BOY: I'll do it if you hold it.

YAHOO: Just get up there, will ya?!

SHY BOY: I won't do it.

> SHY BOY *goes to leave but* YAHOO *stops him.*

YAHOO: Okay, I'll hold it.

> YAHOO *grabs hold of the ladder,* SHY BOY *accepts the challenge, comes over to climb the ladder and just as he is about to put his leg up,* YAHOO *let's go the ladder and moves away.*

SHY BOY: What are you doing?

YAHOO: When you get up there, I'll hold it.

SHY BOY: No way.

YAHOO: I will.

SHY BOY: I'm not doing it.

> SHY BOY *goes to leave again,* YAHOO *is quick to stop him.*

YAHOO: Okay. I'll hold it.

> YAHOO *grabs hold of the ladder again.* SHY BOY *comes over and starts climbing the ladder.*

SHY BOY: Yeah… alright… see… you're the gutless one…

> SHY BOY*'s foot slips on the ladder and he momentarily grips close to the ladder and looks down, very near to falling.*

YAHOO: Hey, you nearly fell on your arse. You know, if you fall and die in your dreams, you're dead for real. Keep goin'.

> SHY BOY *regains his balance and continues climbing, more frightened the higher he goes. He stops climbing a little further up the ladder.*

SHY BOY: That's enough, eh.

YAHOO: No, hurry up, before you wake up. Keep going.

SHY BOY *continues up the ladder until he reaches the top.*

Okay… Now, let go your hands.

SHY BOY: Fifteen bucks.

YAHOO: Come on, just see if you can.

SHY BOY *is standing on the top rung of the ladder. He slowly releases his hands and looks around at the view. He starts feeling incredibly brave.*

SHY BOY: See… you're the gutless one.

YAHOO: How come you told the cops?

SHY BOY *freezes in terror as* YAHOO *takes one hand away from the ladder.*

SHY BOY: I want to get down.

YAHOO: How come you dobbed me in?

SHY BOY: Mum said—

YAHOO: There was no way they woulda caught us if ya didn't dob us both in.

SHY BOY *starts to panic.*

SHY BOY: Get me down.

YAHOO: I thought you were my friend.

SHY BOY: I am your friend.

YAHOO *now balances the ladder upright with just one finger.*

YAHOO: You're a traitor.

SHY BOY: Don't let go.

YAHOO: Traitor! Traitor! Traitor!

SHY BOY *wakes out of his dream suddenly.* YAHOO *stands listening to him from his own cell, as if* SHY BOY *has been calling out in his sleep.*

You alright?

SHY BOY: Yeah… it's just a dream.

YAHOO: You been screamin' and shoutin' all night.

SHY BOY: No, it's cool… I'm alright.

YAHOO: Well, shut up, you're freakin' me out, okay?! What do you think they'll do to us? Eh? What do you think they'll do?

They both fear the future.

SCENE EIGHT: BAIL

YAHOO *now narrates the story to the audience while remaining within the 'action' of the story he tells.*

YAHOO: Next day, we're in front of a magistrate in a Children's Court. He said this is a real serious case and should be heard by a jury in a couple of months' time. He said that we should never see each other again for the rest of our lives and that our parents have to pay five thousand dollars bail so that we can be let out before the next trial. Five thousand bucks. My parents never had five thousand bucks. His did, so they paid and he was allowed to go home straight away. They told me that I had to stay in gaol some more. Next day, the cop comes into my cell.

QUINN: Your mum's here. She's got your bail money. You can go.

YAHOO: Cop lets me out. And there's mi mum standin' in the corridor. Man, she looked like a mess. I said, 'Where did you get the money from?', and she just walks off. I ask her again, 'Where did ya get the money from?', and she just gets in the car. I get in the car too. I think she's driving me home but she drives straight to this private school joint, and she says, 'Get out'. We both get out of the car. We both go into the Principal's office, Mum starts to fill out a form and then she tells the Principal what I done. She just told him. Principal looks at me like I'm dirt. He says, 'Been in a bit of trouble, have you? Well, there'll be no shenanigans in this school, will there?' I say, 'No sir'. I meet these guys, 'Hey, give us forty cents and I'll do it', 'Come on, forty cents… you said you'd give me the money…' I make a call from a phone booth… 'Yeah, is that my old… is that the school?… Okay, this is real important… There's a big bomb planted!… I'm not gonna tell ya where… Look… it's a huge bomb, okay, you'd better hurry up and call the bomb squad before you get your knickers blown off!'… The secretary shat herself on the phone… hahaha…

QUINN: What do you think you're doing?

YAHOO: It was their fault, they made me do it.

QUINN: You've been warned. You've got a couple of months until the trial. It cost your mum five thousand dollars. Now put a lid on it and stay out of trouble. Understand?

YAHOO: Yeah, I understand.

> QUINN *moves off.*

I got taken back to the Principal and he says I failed the school's trial period or something, so I got expelled on the spot. Mum comes down and picks me up, takes me to mi uncle's place. He's really pissed off. Mum hates me anyway. She says so all the time. Probably because I'm dumb. And I don't like staying home.

> YAHOO *gets a lighter out of his pocket and starts passing the flame over his fingers and hands. He eventually rests the flame on the palm of his hand and sees how long he can keep it there. He endures the flame for a long time, until he stops, his hand burning with pain.*

SCENE NINE: COURT

RUSSO *addresses the audience.*

RUSSO: Three months later, the trial begins.

> SHY BOY *and* YAHOO *enter, hassled by numerous photographers and camera crews.* RUSSO *comes over to cover the boy's faces.*

Cover your faces, don't get your face on camera, put your hood over your face, get outta their way!

> *They get inside the court.* RUSSO *approaches the bailiff.*

Excuse me, can the boys sit in the gallery as opposed to the dock? Thank you, sir. Okay, you blokes, come and sit here, you move up a bit, now you sit next to your mate.

> *He sits the boys down and whispers instructions to them.*

Now, you blokes sit here and don't move, this is your spot. And you can take your hood off your face now, mate.

> RUSSO *finds a seat at the back of the court,* SHY BOY *comes up and joins him. There is an uncomfortable pause as the two settle themselves for the hearing.*

SHY BOY: How long does a trial take?
RUSSO: Some trials can take ages.
SHY BOY: What's the longest a trial's ever gone for?

RUSSO: I dunno.

SHY BOY: What's been ya worst case you been on?

RUSSO: Keep your voice down a bit.

SHY BOY: What's the worst case you been on?

RUSSO: Be quiet, do you want to go and stand up there in the dock in front of everyone?

An uncomfortable pause. RUSSO *resumes his narration.*

The trial took a whole month. They brought in witness after witness after witness after specialists, after psychiatrist, after psychologist, then they dragged out the files from 1942, it went on and on and on, you could tell after a while, the jury had no idea what was goin' on. The young bloke sat next to me most of the time. By the end of the fourth week, he was ready for a nervous breakdown.

RUSSO *resumes the 'action' of the scene.* SHY BOY *is now a nervous mess.*

Look, mate, you reckon you can stop shaking, you're making me feel like it's an earthquake or something, you know what I mean?

SHY BOY: Yeah... okay... I can't... I can't help it...

RUSSO: Okay, just put your hands in your pocket—You want something? I'll get you a drink if you want?

SHY BOY: No.

RUSSO: Something to eat? You probably haven't eaten in days, have you?

SHY BOY: No.

Another longer pause. RUSSO *cannot stand the tension.*

RUSSO: Look, I'll get you a drink.

RUSSO *leaves.* SHY BOY *is left on his own. He shakes uncontrollably.*

SHY BOY: Oh man. Why me?

SHY BOY *'becomes' detective* QUINN *and continues narrating the story to the audience.*

QUINN: After the prosecution wrapped up its case against the boys, the defence lawyer just took hold of the younger one by the arm, led him up to the jury and said, 'This child's future, the child's life is resting in your hands'. The jury retired to make their decision, and the court was adjourned until the following day.

SCENE TEN: THE GREAT DEBATE

QUINN *and* RUSSO *are in a bar.* RUSSO *is watching the races on the TV while* QUINN *is playing a poker machine.*

RUSSO: [*to the barman*] Give us a couple of beers thanks, Frankie. And two packets of those salt and vinegar chips. And can you put it on Quinny's tab?!

QUINN: [*calling from the machine*] Hey, it's your shout.

RUSSO: No, it's your shout.

QUINN: No, I won ten bucks on this machine last night and I bought you and Phil a drink.

RUSSO: No you didn't, put your money on the bar for once and buy a shout.

QUINN: Hey, Phil, didn't I win ten bucks on this machine last night and I bought you and Russo…?

RUSSO: Okay, forget it. Don't worry about the beers, Frankie, put the chips back on the rack, we don't want 'em.

QUINN: [*coming over to the bar*] Right-oh, my shout. Sorry, Frankie, I don't know, mate, he's been like this for days, you try workin' with him.

RUSSO: Oh look, I'm sorry, Frankie, I'm just fifteen years old, I haven't got a clue what I'm doin', where I'm goin', who I'm with, you got to excuse all my actions.

QUINN: Oh, come on, Russo, it's the same as the kids who set fire to buildings, same as the kids train surfing…

RUSSO: They're not the same.

QUINN: Same as the kid pulling the chair from under someone and laughing at them falling on their bum.

YAHOO: They're not the same. The kid train surfing is gonna kill himself. The one who pulls the chair out, if that kid falls and breaks his back, or dies, the one who slid the chair out should be held responsible, especially if he's thirteen, or fifteen, that's old enough to know that's a stupid act. They should wear the consequences of that stupidity.

QUINN: Well go on, lock 'em up for fifteen years for pulling a chair out from under someone.

RUSSO: I'm not talkin' about their punishment, I'm talking about whether or not they are guilty, and as far as I'm concerned, at thirteen and fifteen, they're guilty.

SHY BOY: And all I'm tryin' to say to you is that these kids made a mistake.

RUSSO: Oh, that's crap. They knew what they were doing.

SHY BOY: They're average kids like you and I were once…

RUSSO: [*sarcastic*] Oh, well, if they're 'average', then let 'em off. If they were two black kids you'd lock them up, wouldn't you?

QUINN: That's not what I'm saying.

RUSSO: Yes you are, and if one of those kids puts bullets into a gun, goes to a playground, blows a few people away, you'd call that 'a mistake'.

QUINN: I'm not sayin' that.

> RUSSO *turns to a few friends also drinking at the bar.*

RUSSO: Hey, Phil, this guy reckons these kids are too young to know what they're doing therefore we should let them off. How old is your nipper? Eleven? Okay, do you reckon a kid of eleven knows what he's doing? You reckon a kid of eleven knows the difference between right and wrong? If you were on the jury for these boys Phil, would you vote guilty?

> *Phil votes yes.*

Alright, leave your hand up, Phil… Sandy, come here…

QUINN: Sandy's pissed.

RUSSO: Would you vote guilty?

QUINN: She's been drinking here since four o'clock this afternoon.

RUSSO: There's two-nil. Wayne, put the gun down and come over here?

QUINN: Come on, Russo, this is the wrong place to be doing this…

RUSSO: Three-nil. Frankie?

QUINN: He doesn't know the case.

RUSSO: Guilty or not guilty, Frankie? Thank you. Four-nil. What about you, mate?

QUINN: We're talking about two kids' lives…

> *The argument develops into a voting situation with everyone in the pub being asked to vote yes or no. The actors improvise this argument until* QUINN *loses his temper.*

Right-oh, why don't you and your vigilante mates go out in the street, take a rope out of the car, take the two boys down to the main square and hang them, go on, that's what you want to do, isn't it? Hang them. And you can call up their parents on your mobile and get them to come and watch.

QUINN's outburst stops the whole pub, everyone turning to look at him. There is an uncomfortable pause.

RUSSO: What if it was your father in the car? What if it was your mother in the car, and she gets a rock through the chest and kills her, and your beeper goes off now and you and I have to go down to the morgue and identify your own mother's body lying on that slab. What would you think then? That it was an 'accident'? A 'mistake'.

Small pause as RUSSO has made his point quite clear.

QUINN: And what if it was your ten-year-old girl who was up there on the bridge and threw the rock? And she came home and said, 'Dad, I've just killed a man driving a car on the freeway'. What would you do then? Your own kid.

Long pause. QUINN leaves the bar.

RUSSO: Well, we're gonna find out tomorrow, aren't we? You can put your hand down now, Phil.

SCENE ELEVEN: THE VERDICT

RUSSO *and* SHY BOY *are in court.* RUSSO *addresses the audience.*

RUSSO: The next day, we're back in court, waiting for the jury, and the verdict. As usual, the courtroom is packed, and as usual, the young bloke stands next to me. His father never came to the trial. Finally the jury arrive, they take their place. The judge enters and everyone stands. The judge then asks the head juror to read out the verdict… 'For manslaughter and six separate counts of recklessly endangering life… not guilty'.

Pause. SHY BOY lets out a huge release of tension and surprise. He throws his arms around RUSSO and starts crying. RUSSO helps SHY BOY contain himself enough to face the judge.

The judge said, 'These boys have been through enough'. He said 'that they could go home now'… that 'they were free'.

RUSSO becomes YAHOO, smiles broadly and begins leaving the court. Before he exits he looks back at SHY BOY and gives him a thumbs up, a sign of victory. SHY BOY returns the thumbs up reluctantly. YAHOO leaves. SHY BOY then addresses the audience.

SHY BOY: During the trial, there was a woman who sat up the back. She was on her own. She didn't speak to anyone. She wasn't there at the end to hear what happened to us. She was the wife of the guy I killed in the car.

The sounds of wind starts, as was heard during the Prologue.

SHY BOY *walks slowly back to the freeway overpass bridge. He stands and looks down at the traffic. The wind gets stronger. He stands there for a long time, contemplating suicide. As the wind picks up strength, he scares himself with his thoughts and memories and walks away.*

Music starts.

The boys play a final emotive tune together on guitar, not looking at one another.

THE END

From left: Lindy Sardelic as Suzie, Stefo Nantsou as Oscar and Tom Lycos as Kyle in the 2009 Zeal Theatre production of BURNT. *(Photo: Tracy Schramm)*

BURNT

INTRODUCTION:
'A RIPPING YARN'

In the front bar of the local pub in a small country town a bloke tells a ripping yarn to his mate and the barmaid. The tale is full of adventure, history, opinion, local knowledge, and peppered with jokes and gags galore. He even sheds a tear or two as he recounts a few personal details into the mix. His impersonations of characters and events are hilarious and his mate and the barmaid laugh and cry with recognition. Locust plagues, economic downturns, sub-soil moisture, vicious rumours, family hassles and, of course, the bloody drought.

Burnt was born and bred out of the true stories of people from regional Australia struggling with prolonged dryness, and in particular how the stresses and strains of continued drought impacts on families and young people. The play is inspired by that 'bush yarn' quality and the Zeal Theatre style of performance aims to be like that bloke telling a story to his mates in the local bar.

Burnt was originally commissioned by Sydney Theatre Company in 2009, the fourth commission we received after *Gronks*, *Australia v South Africa* and *Taboo*. The commission was made possible through the support of the Girgensohn Foundation and we would like to thank Thomas and Ingeborg Girgensohn for their warmth and enthusiasm for our work. *Burnt* was Zeal Theatre's forty-first production and celebrated our twentieth year since establishment in 1989.

We would like to thank the wonderful students and staff of Wade High School who helped us enormously with the development of the script, as well as Lindy Sardelic, Elliott Weston and Dean Mason who worked on the original staging of the play. We would also like to thank Peter Kenny from AgForce and Helen Hristofski, Cate Blanchett and Andrew Upton at Sydney Theatre Company for sparking this particular project.

Tom Lycos and Stefo Nantsou
December 2010

FIRST PRODUCTION

Burnt premiered at Bega RSL Club, Bega, NSW, on 17 June 2009 with the following cast:

ACTOR 1	Lindy Sardelic
ACTOR 2	Tom Lycos
ACTOR 3	Stefo Nantsou

Directed by Stefo Nantsou with original music by Tom Lycos

A season followed at Sydney Theatre Company 24 June–3 July 2009

CHARACTERS

ACTOR 1:

SUZIE PETRO, 42, farmer
CASEY PETRO, Suzie's daughter, Year Ten student
SANDIE MICKELTON, Casey's best friend, Year Ten student
LAURA WILSEN, 55, farmer
VALERIE PURINE, 60, bitter ex-shop owner
WENDY SNODGRASS, 88, pensioner
FRAN WHIPPLE, 35, hairdresser
AMBER WEEKES, Year Three student
CAROL SATTLER, Royal Hotel barmaid
DEBBIE DALLAS, local policewoman
MISS PIERCE, school principal

ACTOR 2:

KYLE PETRO, Casey's twin brother, Year Ten student
TOBY SATAN, two-year-old child from hell
STEWART CAPELAND, hardware store owner
BRONWYN BOWTELL, Country Women's Association member
MIRIANA GODOLFIS, supermarket check-out girl
FATHER SPANIAL, priest
CAMERON MCKENZIE, Casey's friend, Year Ten student
WARREN BLUFF, real estate agent
DOUG WATKINS, 45, farmer
ALEX DALEY, Year Three student
WEAZEL LOGAN, 82, retired farmer
BILL CHANG, general store owner

ACTOR 3:

GEORGE PETRO, 45, farmer

COLIN KALM, Little Munchkins Child Care worker

RANJIT SINGH, new farmer from India

ALFIE SHRAPNEL, old farmer

MAGGIE COLLINGWOOD, Country Women's Association member

MILES WOODCOCK, menswear manager

GRAHAM LANDFILL, 75, Rotary Club member

OSCAR PARKER, Kyle's friend, Year Ten student

MR O'DANIELS, high school Science teacher

CHARLIE SELMAN, auctioneer

PROLOGUE

Music starts. As music fades, the actor playing CASEY *steps forward.*

CASEY: My name's Casey Petro. We live on a farm near a small town called Gilpendry about six hundred and fifty kilometres [*pointing*] that way. Our property's called 'Eureka' and we got heaps of sheep and grow fruit. I live there with my dad… [*imitating him*] everyone calls him Lee Kernaghan 'cause of his cowboy hat; my mum… [*imitating her*] she always keeps heaps busy and scurries around like a chook; and my twin brother Kyle… [*imitating him*] he doesn't say much and plays *Call of Duty 5* all day. I'm twenty-three minutes older than him and it really shows. We're in Year Ten. We go to school in town 'bout fifteen ks outta Gilpendry.

When I was little we used to play hide and seek in amongst the orange trees, now they're barely over our knees. In our backyard we always put up a pool, it was sweet as, so since the drought's gone worse, it started getting smaller, and now we don't have it.

Our lawn's dead.

Everyone's garden's dead.

It happens really fast, you don't really notice it.

This is our story.

ACT ONE: UNHINGED

SCENE ONE: THE FARM (SUNRISE)

Eureka. Early morning. GEORGE *and* SUZIE *are herding livestock through a gate. There are constant sound effects of sheep, dogs, whistling, flies—a hot and humid morning at the start of a long hard day.*

SUZIE *goes into the barn and gets some saddlery and tools, which she then hands over to* GEORGE.

GEORGE: Don't forget to go to Capelands' for that wire. And see if he's got any brass hinges for that lower gate. We need about four sets. Or at least two. Whatever he's got.

SUZIE: I'll see how much they are.

> *The dog barks.*

GEORGE: Benny's still limping.

SUZIE: Yeah… I'll see if I can get some bandages… or something. Anything else you want while I'm in town?

> GEORGE *shakes his head.*

GEORGE: Come on, kids, Kyle, Casey!

SUZIE: Get in the car… hurry up! [*To* GEORGE] See ya tonight, then.

GEORGE: See ya.

> GEORGE *leaves, herding the animals.* SUZIE *looks up at the sky, shading her eyes from the beautiful sunrise. Music starts.*

SCENE TWO: SCHOOL DROP-OFF

SUZIE *is driving the twins to school,* CASEY *beside her and* KYLE *in the back seat.*

SUZIE: Just stop your whining, Kyle, will ya, mate, and put your seatbelt on, we're comin' into town… the last thing we need is some two-hundred-dollar fine, and Senior Constable Houston or what's-her-name won't take your flimsy excuse that it was your turn to sit in the front. And you, Miss, can stop blowing ya hair out of your face, it's so annoying. We all know if you 'had a GHD you wouldn't be blowing your horrible hair so much', I've heard that one before too, and it don't wash.

She drives past a friend and waves a 'hello'.

I got my meetings today, so I can do the pick-up after school. I'll see Miles about your suit for the formal, Kyle... he said he'd see if he could get that really nice dark blue one with the buttons, the one we saw in the catalogue...? No, no, you are not wearing a light orange retro number, I won't have you sticking out like dogs' balls.

She puts the blinker on, turns a corner, and parks outside the school.

Right, now I gave you the money for the excursion, didn't I? Good. And that envelope with the cheque in it for your school photos... you got both yours and Kyle's... don't forget to hand them in please. Okay, see you later, have a nice day.

KYLE *and* CASEY *have gotten out of the car and are walking away.*

And Casey? Ask Mr O'Daniels what you have to take on the excursion, what bedding you might need... Okay, see yas this arvo.

SUZIE *has a headache, looks at her watch and realises she's late, goes to drive off but there's the morning traffic jam around the school.*

Come on, move it, you old goat...

SCENE THREE: LITTLE MUNCHKINS CHILD CARE CENTRE

Twelve minutes later, at the Little Munchkins Child Care Centre, SUZIE *arrives to see two-year-old* TOBY *running around the centre screaming 'Running amok, running amok, running amok'. Child care worker* COLIN KALM *enters, holding a screaming baby.*

TOBY: I'm running amok, Colin!
COLIN: You sure are, Toby... [*To* SUZIE] Yes, can I help you?
SUZIE: Hi, arh, my name's Suzie...
COLIN: Toby. Calm down, mate. [*To* SUZIE] Sorry...
SUZIE: Suzie, Suzie Petro, I had a nine o'clock appointment...

The phone rings.

... with, arh... Helen...

COLIN: Sorry...

COLIN *answers the phone, still holding the crying baby.*

Hello, Little Munchkins Child Care Centre... Hi, Jane... Yeah, she's fine...

The baby screams louder.

Not a peep out of her... Okay, we'll see you round four... Thanks, Jane... 'Bye.

SUZIE: I'm a little late... I'm sorry...

TOBY: Running a total muck...

COLIN: Toby...

SUZIE: She said she'd see me first thing this morning...

COLIN: Helen's, arh... excuse me... Toby mate... go into the 'Blue Tongue' room, Gale is about to read a story.

TOBY: No, no, no, I'm running amok, I'm running amok... I don't like Gale...

SUZIE: [*trying to keep it together as the baby screams louder*] I wanted to see her about...

COLIN: I'm sorry, who did you want to see?

SUZIE: Arh, Helen... Baker? Is it? I wanted to see if—

COLIN: You mean Piper.

SUZIE: Piper, sorry...

TOBY: I want some warm juice in a bottle, warm juice in a bottle...

COLIN: Helen's just gone to a meeting... Toby!

SUZIE: She said I could come in today to see about a part-time job...

TOBY: [*suddenly crying*] I wet myself! Errrrrrrrrrr...

The baby that COLIN *is holding vomits all down* COLIN*'s back and cries louder.*

COLIN: Excuse me...

COLIN *gives* SUZIE *the screaming baby and goes over to* TOBY. SUZIE *stands uncomfortably holding the baby which is covered in vomit and has obviously soiled itself.*

TOBY: Colin... I wet myself...

COLIN: Toby... Toby, listen... mate, go to the 'Blue Tongue' room. Gale's got some squishy banana.

TOBY: [*suddenly stopping*] Squishy 'nana?

COLIN: A lot of squishy banana... go and see.

TOBY: [*instantly overjoyed*] Yay, squishy banana, I'm gonna squash squishy banana in Gale's hair... I'll run amok with squishy banana... [*Running off*] Yeah! Gale... I wet myself.

COLIN: Now... sorry... you're here for a part-time job, that is excellent, look, I'll tell Helen you came... arh, what was your name again?

Small pause. SUZIE *thinks twice about this idea.*

SUZIE: It's okay.

She holds the baby out to COLIN.

Don't worry about it.

SCENE FOUR: CAPELANDS' HARDWARE

Twenty minutes later, SUZIE *waits at Capelands' hardware store while* STEWART CAPELAND *is serving* RANJIT SINGH, *a new farmer to the area.*

SINGH: I'm trying not to worry about it, I'm trying very, very hard, but I'm also trying to contact the Water Board about it and they tell me that if I have to buy water, I would be better to buy it locally and save on the freight costs...

STEWART: Well, that is true, but arh...

SINGH: I know it's true, I know it for a fact, but why do they keep me waiting on the phone for one whole hour to tell me something I already know? Tell me, why?

STEWART: [*seeing* SUZIE] I'll be with you in a sec, Suzie...

SUZIE: No worries.

SINGH: To freight it in or buy it locally it will still cost me very, very expensive...

STEWART: You got room for more tanks on your property...

SINGH: There's plenty of room... but not enough water.

STEWART: Why don't you have a look at the tanks then, they're just out there... I got a few sizes you can pick from...

SINGH: What is the point of buying more tanks unless they are filled with water?

STEWART: Look, mate, I'll be out there in a minute, I'll just see to this customer…

SINGH: Yes yes, you… see to your customer, I have to think about this now…

SINGH *goes past* SUZIE *and out to see the water tanks.*

STEWART: [*to* SUZIE] You're after that fencing wire, yeah…?

SUZIE *nods and smiles.*

ALFIE: [*standing in the doorway of the store as* SINGH *walks past him*] What is there to think about, mate? If ya ain't got enough water ya gonna go bloody broke. Simple as that.

SUZIE: And how much for a set of brass hinges?

STEWART: The big ones?

SUZIE *nods.* STEWART *goes to have a look.*

ALFIE: [*to* SUZIE] And howsitgoin' with you lot out Gilpendry way? Yous gonna have a decent crop this year?

SUZIE: We're doing it tough, Alfie.

ALFIE: You hear the Walshes are selling up.

SUZIE: No, I didn't know that.

STEWART: I only got three pair left.

SUZIE: I'll take the two.

ALFIE: Well, if ya got some spare water at your place, sell some to Mahatma Gandhi over there.

STEWART: They're eighteen fifty a pair.

ALFIE: At triple the price.

SUZIE: Whatever, Stewart, fine. Who's got spare water, Alfie?

SINGH: [*re-entering*] Do you think the medium size tank would fit in the back of my utility?

STEWART: What sort of ute have you got?

SINGH: [*very proud*] Toyota… HiLux, one of the new ones.

ALFIE: If you can afford a new HiLux, mate, you can afford to fill that tank full of champagne.

SINGH: I don't like champagne. [*To* STEWART] I'll bring the car around the side.

STEWART: Right-oh, mate.

ALFIE: [*under his breath as* SINGH *exits past him*] Smartarse.

STEWART: [*to* SUZIE] Cash or credit?

SUZIE: Credit.

ALFIE: What's the bet Chandrasaka here stacks his HiLux on the roofing tiles.

STEWART: 'Pin' and 'OK'.

SUZIE: Haven't got a part-time job going here, have you, Stewart?

STEWART: Got the mother-in-law working here now. Save me a quid or two. There's your receipt. I'll load that wire into the back of the car for you.

SUZIE: Thanks. If something comes up…

STEWART: Yeah…

ALFIE: Ha, Stewart, look at this… he rammed it straight into a pallet full a fertiliser bags. What a dill. That HiLux'll stink of shit till Christmas. Serves him bloody right too.

> SUZIE *looks at her watch, realises she's late.*

[*Calling out to* SINGH] Good on ya, Mr Bollywood, top effort!

SCENE FIVE: COUNTRY WOMEN'S ASSOCIATION MEETING

Twenty-five minutes later, the Country Women's Association ladies are comparing their cakes for the upcoming cake stall fundraiser.

BRONWYN: And good on you, Mrs Collingwood, that's a terrific effort.

MAGGIE: Well, I was up to four a.m. this morning, but honestly, it wasn't the cooking that was the problem this time… it was Barry… screaming from the bedroom, 'Come to bed, come to bed', and I said, 'No, this is CWA business and you can do without a bit of slap and tickle for one night, you randy old goat!'

> *They all laugh.*

BRONWYN: Alright, so let's have a look shall we… that makes… six pavlovas, five biscuit bakes… four rocky roads, the assorted cream sponges, and of course, Glenda's fabulous Raspberry Swirl, you've done it again, Glenda… In fact I am so tempted to just dip my little pinky in there for a quick taste while no-one's looking… You should have your own TV show, Glenda. 'Glenda's Magic Swirl'.

> *They all laugh again.* SUZIE *stands smiling, embarrassed that she hasn't brought anything with her to this meeting.*

Suzie?

SUZIE: I'm so sorry I'm late, Bron…

BRONWYN: Have you made something for the fundraiser?

SUZIE: Arh… I'm happy to person the stall for a few hours on a Thursday afternoon.

BRONWYN: Well, any assistance is greatly appreciated. Alright, girls, let's go sell some cakes.

SUZIE: [*a little nervous*] Arh… before anyone goes…

> All the ladies stop and stare at SUZIE. Small awkward pause.

BRONWYN: Yes, Suzie?

SUZIE: If anyone knows of arh… a part-time job going… or… arh… [*Small pause.*] Just putting it out there…

> The other ladies just stare at her blankly.

SCENE SIX: SUPERMARKET CHECK-OUT

Two hours later, SUZIE *is at the supermarket check-out. As the check-out girl is bipping all the items through,* SUZIE *is wondering if she could do that job. There are many bips before the final price is given.*

MIRIANA: Eighy-eight dollars seventy-six.

> SUZIE *gives her the credit card.*

Credit?

> SUZIE *nods.*

FlyBuys?

> SUZIE *shakes her head.*

Cash out?

> SUZIE *shakes her head.*

'Pin' and 'OK' please.

> SUZIE *types in her pin.* MIRIANA *gives her the reciept.*

Thank you very much, have a happy day.

SUZIE: You… have a happy day too.

SCENE SEVEN: MENSWEAR

One hour later, SUZIE *is at the menswear store.* MILES *brings on the suit for Kyle's formal.*

MILES: So you're happy with this one?

SUZIE: Very happy, thank you, Miles.

MILES: I think your son will look a million dollars in this one, I really do... and these buttons match his eyes, don't you think? I remember last time he was in the shop Kyle was talking about wearing some sort of light orange retro number? I don't think so... I don't think any girl would be caught dead with a boy dressed like that, do you?! I think this one is a lot more appropriate. Has he got a date yet?

SUZIE: I don't think so.

MILES: What about your daughter, what's her name?

SUZIE: Casey.

MILES: Casey, right, what's she wearing on the big night?

SUZIE: Yeah, she can't make up her mind, as usual... She just wants what's most expensive. They might be twins but they're certainly not identical.

MILES: Well, I'll keep Kyle's suit here, and you can pick it up anytime after one o'clock on the day of the formal.

SUZIE: Okay. [*Small pause.*] Miles... You run this shop on your own... Doesn't it ever get very busy...?

MILES: Busy? In this town? I don't think so. Luckily this building's been in the family for generations, otherwise I honestly wouldn't make enough to pay the rent. Now, would you like to put a deposit on that?

She hands him her credit card.

Thank you. Savings or credit?

SUZIE: Arh... credit.

MILES: 'Pin' and 'OK'.

She types the numbers and presses 'OK'. Pause. It is not approved. SUZIE *stands very embarrassed.*

Let's try it again.

MILES *swipes the card and repeats the process.*

'Pin' and 'OK'.

SUZIE *types in her pin again and once again the pause is excruciating and uncomfortable as she waits for the approval.* SUZIE*'s face shows the result.*

Perhaps you're over your limit today?

MILES *hands back her credit card.*

Might be worth a trip to the bank?

SUZIE *smiles meekly.*

SCENE EIGHT: ROTARY CLUB MEETING

Twenty minutes later, SUZIE *is at the Rotary Club meeting listening to* FATHER SPANIAL *who is wrapping up his presentation to the members.*

SPANIAL: … and that's my trip to Belgium.

The Rotarians clap FATHER SPANIAL*'s presentation.*

GRAHAM: Thank you, Father Spanial, I had no idea they called it Antwerpen, I thought it was called Antwerp. Fancy that… eh?

SPANIAL: And, I'd like to put in a special request if I may, Graham, I think it would be nice if we displayed the Antwerpen Rotary Club's banner next to the ones we've already got from Stamsund in Norway and Hellevetislous from the Netherlands, and keep all the European ones together.

GRAHAM: That's a wonderful idea, Father, all the European banners in the corner there… All those in favour? Against? I declare it carried. How about another round of applause for Father Spanial and his Belgian report.

The members clap FATHER SPANIAL *as he sits down next to* SUZIE.

You're our very own Billy Connolly you are, Father, you've certainly travelled all over the shop… you should grow your hair long and one of them goaties and paint it purple like he does… [*He laughs at his own joke.*] Okay, everyone, settle down… We have one last agenda item before we break for afternoon tea kindly donated by Stevie Magann and the Gun Club, thanks Stevie, the Gunners have been big supporters for the Rotary Club over the years, good to see you out of hospital, and, arh, your leg is lookin' a lot better, mate. Now, this is a very unusual request from a Rotary exchange student from the United Arab Emirates. We've never had anyone come out from there before... I'm sure that'll raise a few eyebrows in the community... Mind you, it does say on the request form that the lad is Christian, not Muslim, I didn't know there were any Christians in the Middle East...

SPANIAL: [*whispering to* SUZIE] Are you alright, Suzie?

SUZIE: Yes, Father... everything's fine. [*Small pause.*] Father, do you have someone who comes in and... arh... cleans the church or... does the odd job around the, the... you know...?

SPANIAL: One of the parishioners comes in once a week, Wendy Snodgrass, you know Wendy? She gives it a bit of a vacuum and a dust over.

SUZIE: Right... I was just... in case you needed a hand...

SPANIAL: Oh, Wendy's a pain in the proverbial, but she's actually very good. Thanks for offering.

SUZIE: [*looking at her watch*] No worries... I have to go... Pick-up time.

SUZIE *stands to leave.*

GRAHAM: What about you, Suzie?

SUZIE *stops and stares at* GRAHAM *like a rabbit at an oncoming truck.*

You want a nice Arab boy on your property for the next two years?

SUZIE: [*smiling meekly*] I'll give it some thought, Graham.

SCENE NINE: SCHOOL PICK-UP

After school, KYLE *and his friend,* OSCAR, *are sitting waiting in the car.* SUZIE *arrives.*

SUZIE: Sorry I'm late.

KYLE: Can we give Oscar a lift home, Mum?

SUZIE: No worries. Hi, Oscar.

OSCAR: Hey, Mrs Petro. S'up?

SUZIE: Where's your sister?

KYLE: Formal committee meeting. She's going to Sandie's place and getting a lift home later. Did you order mi suit?

SUZIE: [*knowing she hasn't*] Arh... yeah.

OSCAR: What sort of suit ya gettin'?

KYLE: This posh, dark blue one, straight as.

OSCAR: I'm wearing this light orange retro suit mi dad wore to his formal… he's even got the pink shirt with the frills here and the green velvet bow tie, looks awesome. I'm not allowed to wear it to the afterparty but, Mum reckons I'll spew all over it, she's probably right, I told 'em they should insure it against damages, be worth over nine hundred dollars, but I don't reckon you can insure something against your own son, eh, anyway, at least I know what I'm wearin'. Totes sorted.

SUZIE: That sounds really good, Oscar.

KYLE: [*knowing his mum is being sarcastic*] Yeah right.

Small pause. OSCAR *sees someone out the car window.*

OSCAR: [*yelling*] Hey, Cameron, get a life, ya tool. [*He turns to* KYLE] Kelly's gonna drop him, she told me at lunchtime, eh, sweet, I'll move in on her on the rebound.

KYLE: Yeah right.

Small pause.

SUZIE: Hey, Oscar, does your mum still do the cleaning at the school?

OSCAR: Nar… she barred it… Once she had to clean the boys toilets that was enough for her… She reckons you gotta get paid ten thousand bucks just to walk into the boys toilets and then double that to get down on your hands and knees with a toilet brush.

KYLE: Oooooo.

OSCAR: I agreed with her. Dad called her weak. Harsh.

Small pause.

SUZIE: So… who does that job now?

OSCAR: I dunno… some Pakistani woman… [*To* KYLE] Where she's from…?

KYLE: I dunno.

Another small pause.

SUZIE: So… what's your mum do now?

OSCAR: Nothin'. Helps Dad with his septic tank business. Hey, just drop me on the corner, Mrs Petro. I'll walk from here. Thanks for the lift. Later, dude.

KYLE: Later.

SUZIE *pulls over,* OSCAR *jumps out of the car, they drive off again. Small pause.*

What's for dinner?

SUZIE: [*exasperated*] I don't know, Kyle, I haven't thought that far ahead. I'm sure when we get home and I unpack all the bags I'll be able to cobble together something that I'm sure even you might find edible, and if it isn't good enough for you then you can start cooking for yourself, how does that sound? [*Pause.*] Probably spaghetti. That good enough for you?

KYLE: Only asking.

SCENE TEN: HOME

They arrive home. KYLE *leaps out of the car leaving* SUZIE *to get all the shopping bags herself.*

SUZIE: Kyle?!

He doesn't respond and exits. SUZIE *brings all the shopping into the kitchin and starts putting things away in the refrigerator and the cupboards.* GEORGE *enters and starts washing his hands. By now* SUZIE *is fuming.*

GEORGE: Did you get the hinges?

SUZIE: Spaghetti.

GEORGE: What?

SUZIE: I put a packet of Tim Tams back on the shelf because I thought it was too extravagant. I couldn't pay the rent on Kyle's suit either. Do you know how embarrassing it is when it comes up 'Transaction Denied', and I didn't have a cent in my purse and I know the petrol gauge is just about on 'Empty'? And I couldn't give a hoot how you pronounce Antwerp, I know I can't make a raspberry swirl as good as Glenda Golfbuggy or whatever her name is, and I don't want squishy banana smeared through my hair. And I ain't getting down on my hands and knees and scrubbing out the boys' toilets at school, it's bad enough I have to scrub out our own toilet every second day, but I can't do that. I can put up with a lot, but I can't do that. [*She slams the hinges down on the table.*] The hinges were eighteen fifty a pair, I only got the two. [*Small pause.*] I think I'm the one who needs them. [*Suddenly realising*] Oh… and I didn't get the bandage for Benny's leg either… I just forgot…

GEORGE: I ripped up an old shirt for Benny's leg. It's fine. It's all gonna be just fine. [*Small pause.*] The near-side crop's doin' okay. Far-side's a bit iffy, but we only need a drop or two of rain and that might be okay too. Could get not a bad harvest if we're lucky. Fingers crossed. Fingers and toes. So just relax.

SUZIE: [*loudly*] Yes… I'm very relaxed, George… I'm totally and utterly relaxed.

GEORGE: [*snapping loudly*] Alright, you don't have to get squishy banana through your hair if you don't want to, okay, forget it, just sit home all day and watch the tele, don't worry about it. [*Small tense pause.*] Tim Tams are overrated. [*He grabs the hinges.*] I'll put these hinges on the back gate before it gets too dark. Forget about dinner for me, I'm not hungry now.

> GEORGE *leaves.* SUZIE *stands in the kitchen very depressed.*

SCENE ELEVEN: LOCUST PLAGUE

GEORGE *goes into the shed, grabs some tools and prepares to fix the gate.*

GEORGE: Benny… outta there… get out.

> GEORGE *starts to fix the gate with the new hinges.*
>
> *The mood gets suddenly very dark.*
>
> *There is a locust plague on the horizon, and without warning, suddenly swarms through the property.*

Suzie! Get the tarp… we'll do the tractor first…

> *The noise is shockingly loud and irritating.* SUZIE *comes out of the house and they both unravel a huge tarpaulin and cover up the tractor.*

Get the windows on the car… and in the house, hurry up…

> SUZIE *dashes for the car and exits into the house in a panic to get everything closed from the locusts.* GEORGE *tries to cover things up but is overcome by the numbers of locusts swarming all over him. Everything goes into slow motion as the noise of the locusts gets louder and louder… until fading as* CASEY *steps forward.*

CASEY: [*narrating*] When the swarm of locust comes over, millions of them, it's like a big black cloud coming over the horizon and you think, here we go again... Wasn't the first time. But this time it was right on picking time... Wiped out the crop... They ate everything. Everything gone. There won't be a harvest this season.

END OF ACT ONE

ACT TWO: RESPECT

SCENE ONE: SCHOOL

The next day, OSCAR *and* KYLE *are at school.*

OSCAR: Dude, Dad wouldn't pull over, he just kept on driving, had the wipers goin' full blast and everything, flicking all these locusts off, couldn't hardly see the road, we nearly died about twelve times, it was awesome.

KYLE: Least I won't have to help with the harvest this year.

CASEY: [*entering*] Where were youse in History?

KYLE: We had to… arh…

OSCAR: Miss Freiling asked us to help her out in the multi-purpose centre, we had to set up chairs for some stupid drama thing from Sydney.

CASEY: That is so lame, Oscar.

OSCAR: It's true, I swear to God. Go ask her.

KYLE: Did O'Daniels chuck a fit?

CASEY: We got our marks back for the White Australia Policy report.

OSCAR: Oh yeah, how'd ya go?

CASEY: Eighteen out of twenty.

OSCAR: Oooo, rocket scientist.

CASEY: You got ten out of twenty.

OSCAR: Ten? Neither a pass nor a fail, that's pure borderline, dude, awesome!

CASEY: [*handing* KYLE *his report*] Here's yours.

> KYLE *grabs it but doesn't read the result.*

OSCAR: What d'you get?

> OSCAR *goes to grab it but* KYLE *doesn't let him.*

CASEY: He got two.

OSCAR: Two?

CASEY: Yep. Two.

OSCAR: Two out of twenty? Dude, that's an all-time low. Congratulations.

> KYLE *reads his report.*

CASEY: And Mr O'Daniels said he got that much because he at least spelt his name right.

OSCAR *laughs at the gag.*

O'Daniels told me to tell ya you better start showing up to class again. You're heading for your second N Award. Three strikes and you don't get your School Certificate.

KYLE: So what?

CASEY: So what, I'm just being the messenger.

OSCAR: In ancient Greece they used to cut off the head of the messenger who brought bad news.

CASEY: Well, text me when you want to cut off my head, Oscar, ya tool. And you should get some chewing gum or Soothers or something. You both stink of pot.

She walks away.

KYLE: Hey, Sis.

CASEY: What?

KYLE *raises the finger. She repeats the gesture back and leaves.*

OSCAR: Hey, what if I asked your sister to the formal?

KYLE: First, I'd glass ya in the face, then I'd cut your eyes out with a compass, slash your dick and balls off and feed 'em to a dog, pour petrol over what's left of ya and then set you on fire. And then I'd kill ya.

OSCAR: So that's a no go. [*Small pause.*] Who you gonna ask, dude?

SANDIE MICKLETON *enters.*

SANDIE: Hey.

KYLE: Hey.

OSCAR: Hey, it's the Sandie! S'up?

SANDIE: [*to* KYLE] Seen ya sister?

OSCAR: [*answering for* KYLE] Yeah, she was just here, you goin' to touch footy later?

SANDIE: Youse'd get thrashed without me.

OSCAR: [*starting to shadow box with her*] Gonna start another punch up, are ya, Sandie the thugster? Get an all-in goin'.

SANDIE: [*punching back*] I might.

KYLE: Who's goin' to Pintoon Park after?

SANDIE *grabs* OSCAR *around the neck in a headlock.*

SANDIE: Everyone.

OSCAR: Ow…

SANDIE: You?

KYLE: Probs.

SANDIE: Had enough, Oscar?

OSCAR: Yes.

SANDIE *lets him go.*

Man… you gonna need a good lawyer. That hurts now.

SANDIE: You need some chewy or a Soother or something.

OSCAR: Yeah, right.

MR O'DANIELS *enters.*

O'DANIELS: Where were you two last period?

OSCAR: Arh… Mr O'Daniels, we were helping Miss Freiling put out the chairs in the multi-purpose hall for some drama thing, sir. Hey… we told Miss Freiling we didn't want to miss your History lesson class, didn't we, we told her straight, but she was very insistent, sir. She can be very persuasive, sir, that Miss Freiling.

O'DANIELS: Well, that is very interesting, Oscar, given that Miss Frieling is away today. And what about you, Kyle? What's your excuse this time?

KYLE: Don't have one.

O'DANIELS: Well, that's short and sweet, a lot like your report… at least it's a little more honest. Sandie here could probably tell me more about the White Australia Policy than you could and she doesn't even do History. Isn't that right, Sandie?

SANDIE: Don't think so, sir. Never heard of it.

O'DANIELS: Pity. And a pity you can't join us on the excursion next month.

SANDIE: I go to Sydney heaps, sir.

O'DANIELS: Is that a fact? Experienced the Parliament House tour? Been around the Rocks? Gone to the Powerhouse Museum?

SANDIE: No, we go every year to watch the Swans play.

O'DANIELS: Fair enough. Well, the Swannies'll need to lift their game if they're to have any hope this year. Much like you, Kyle.

KYLE: I don't like the Swans.

O'DANIELS: Why can't you be more like your sister? Eh? It's not too late to get your head out of your ar... to show some improvement.

Small pause, no response.

OSCAR: You nearly said 'arse', sir...

O'DANIELS: Oscar, you stink. Go get some chewing gum... or a Soother or something, you both smell like you've been up the oval bonging on all morning. [*Small pause.*] Don't get too close to this pair, Sandie, you're likely to catch some exotic disease.

SANDIE: Yes, sir.

O'DANIELS: [*noticing a few boys on the other side of the oval*] Hey, you lot, stop stuffing garbage down that boy's shirt, cut it out...

O'DANIELS *leaves.*

KYLE: Prick.

SANDIE: Tool.

OSCAR: Man, I should sue him for defamation of character, how dare he insinuate we been smoking pot all morning. Was only a half hour. Youse got two bucks, I'll go get some chewy.

KYLE: No.

SANDIE: Go ask Cameron, he's usually got some.

OSCAR: Good idea. Later, dudes. Hey, Cameron, S'up...?

OSCAR *leaves. Small pause.*

SANDIE: Youse get much damage at your place?

OSCAR: Yeah.

Tiny pause.

SANDIE: Hear Madison's oldies are movin?

KYLE: Na.

SANDIE: Might be goin' to Melbourne.

KYLE: Melbourne?

SANDIE: She's devo, should see her. When we moved here I thought this town was huge, but Melbourne, Geez. [*Small pause.*] Got your suit for the formal?

KYLE: Yeah.

Small pause. There is an obvious tension between them.

It's blue.

Another pause.

SANDIE: So... I'll see you this arvo at touch footy?

KYLE: Yeah.

> SANDIE *smiles and leaves. Pause.*

> KYLE *reads his report and then rips it to pieces.*

> *Music starts.*

SCENE TWO: TOUCH FOOTY

KYLE *simulates a game of touch football, tenaciously going for his opponents.*

OSCAR *and* SANDIE *are on the sideline cheering their team on.*

Then OSCAR *runs on and joins in the game.* OSCAR *is slower and more sluggish.*

Then SANDIE *joins them. She is very good at the game.*

The game builds in intensity. This sequence ends with a slow motion intercept try by SANDIE *which wins them the game. The whole team then lift her up in triumph.*

SCENE THREE: PINTOON PARK

Later that night in Pintoon Park it is pitch black. KYLE *is using the light on his mobile phone to see where he is going.*

KYLE: Hey, Oscar? Cameron? Where are yas?

VOICES: Piss off... Get lost, Petro, ya wanker... Turn ya phone off, ya jerk!

KYLE: Yeah yeah, youse all piss off, get out of it!

OSCAR: Hey, Kyle, we're over here.

> *The lights slowly come up on* OSCAR *who is sitting drinking beer with a few mates.*

What d'ya get?

KYLE: [*holding up a bottle*] Vodka.

OSCAR: Stolichnaya! Russian *wodka*! Top shelf variety, dude, where d'you get it from?

> KYLE *hands* OSCAR *the bottle and he has a big drink.*

KYLE: Royal bottlo… that barmaid chick was in the front bar… didn't see me come through the carpark.

OSCAR: Stealth… Well, while you were gone me and Douglas the Cutlass and Angus the Mighty Burger… we are polishing off a slab, eh boys!

KYLE: [*also drinking straight from the bottle*] Where's Sandie?

OSCAR: She's gone.

KYLE: What?

OSCAR: Hey, what was all that crap with O'Daniels today, he's a total… like…

They keep drinking the vodka.

KYLE: He's got it in for me is what he is…

OSCAR: What you need to do is treat him like… he sends you a message… and you ignore him…

KYLE: I do ignore him.

OSCAR: … and then you block him…

KYLE: I do block him.

OSCAR: … and then you de-friend him…

KYLE: He's not my friend. I hate him. I want to punch the guy in the face.

The sound of a train going past is heard. It's a regular sight every Wednesday night.

The nine forty-five. Right on time.

OSCAR: Man, we should be on that train. Where's it go?

KYLE: You want to be on a train and you don't know where it goes?

OSCAR: Well, it's going east… so that's either to Sydney or the Coast or somewhere good.

KYLE: That's west, ya tool.

OSCAR: No it ain't.

KYLE: Yes it is.

OSCAR: Well, whatever, I like trains. They stay on the rails. My mum says I can do whatever as long as I stay on the rails, and I tell her I'll drive trains.

OSCAR *laughs at his lame gag.*

KYLE: Where's Sandie?

OSCAR: She got picked up by someone, you just missed her.

KYLE: Who?

OSCAR: I dunno, someone came and she went off with them.

KYLE: Who was it?

OSCAR: Dunno. Didn't see who it was, she just saw the light, knew who it was and took off. Said she'll see ya tomorrow at school, if you go, that is.

KYLE: What sort of car did they have?

OSCAR: I don't know what sort of car… it was definitely a car with two working headlights, so that should narrow it down… But whoever it was is, like, totally in love with Sandie, and I could tell by the look on her, how excited she looked… And now you're just standing there like some jealous prick because someone has obviously stolen your sweet Sandie… and you shoulda asked Sandie to the formal quicker, man, while you had the chance, before the mysterious car dude moved in on her… Probably some guy from Year Twelve, or whatshisname, that buff ranger dude…

KYLE: [*exploding*] Why don't you just shut your stupid donut hole right up, Oscar, eh!

> KYLE *grabs the bottle and goes. Pause as* OSCAR *recovers from* KYLE'*s outburst.*

OSCAR: Ooooo… stepped on a cornea… Hey… Angus… any more of that slab left?

> CASEY *enters with her mobile phone light on.*

CASEY: Hey, Kyle… you there? Kyle?

A VOICE: Get lost, Petro!

CASEY: Oooo, sorry. Kyle!

OSCAR: Casey, Casey… yeah, over here through the bushes… S'up?

CASEY: That you, Oscar… Where's Kyle?

OSCAR: You, he was, your brother was just here a second ago, you're always, people are always missing each other…

CASEY: Where'd he go…? Sandie's dad's here, we're getting a lift home in his car.

OSCAR: Sandie's dad's car?

CASEY: Yes, Sandie's dad's car… we been waitin' for Kyle… where is he?

OSCAR: [*realising*] Oh, I've given the wrong, Angus gave your brother the wrong disinformation, see… your brother, he's got the hots for…

oops… shtum… not a word. I dunno nothin' in life. Shut up, Angus, that's a secret.

CASEY: If you see him, tell him I've gone home and he should get himself there too, it's late… Dad's spewin'.

OSCAR: Your dad, Mr Lee Kernaghan with the, the hat… I'll tell him, I'll be the ancient Greek messenger of bad news and he can cut off my head and feed my balls to a dog…

CASEY: See ya, Oscar.

CASEY *leaves.*

OSCAR: Oooooo… it's Sandie's father's car… not the… the mystery… oooooo… chub chub chub chub… [*He becomes more and more incoherent until he vomits everywhere.*] … Hey, Angus… that looks like you. [*He then falls in his own vomit.*] Ohhh… Mum'll clean it.

SCENE FOUR: TRASHING THE ENGLISH-HISTORY STAFFROOM

Twenty-five minutes later, KYLE *breaks into the English-History faculty staffroom and starts trashing the place. He then gathers some papers in a pile and goes to start a fire.*

A torch shines on his face. He looks up and freezes. It's SENIOR CONSTABLE DEBBIE DALLAS.

DALLAS: Hello… is that Casey? Is your mother or father home, Casey? It's Senior Constable Dallas from the police station in town… could I speak with your… Thank you. [*Small pause.*] Hello, George… it's Debbie Dallas here, um, sorry to ring you at this hour, I figured I'd make the call first before I made the trek out there… Arh… I've got your son down here at the station… No, he's fine, he's had a bit too much to drink by the look of him, by his appearance… Arh, I caught him at the school, the high school, he was involved in a break and enter situation, and arh, as well as completely trashing the English-History staffroom, he seemed, arh, a little intent on burning the place down if I hadn't've shown up when I did.

I'm gonna have to charge him with the break-in and the malicious damage… If you could come down to the station to pick him up… or I could come and drop him off at yours… whatever's easiest for you…

Pause. The scene starts to shift in slow motion.

No, he was on his own by the look of him... He's not saying very much as you'd expect... not a big talker your lad... coulda been worse... a lot worse of course. [*Small pause.*] No, I don't know what he was thinking.

SCENE FIVE: HOME WAR

The lights come up at the Petro house some two hours later, GEORGE *having picked* KYLE *up and brought him home where he sits in the lounge room, his parents standing looking at him in disgust and disbelief.*

SUZIE: What were you thinking? What, you were gonna burn the whole school down? Because you failed a... an essay or something? Because you failed an exam? You want to be expelled? You'll get at least a temporary... what do they call it... expulsion.

>   KYLE *is silent and brooding.*

Eh? Tell us. We're your parents, Kyle, we have a right to know.

>   *Pause.* SUZIE *looks at* GEORGE *who is too disgusted to talk.*

So, now you're charged, you have to appear in the Children's Court, I suppose we have to arrange legal aid or a solicitor... not to mention the cost of the damages... Jesus Christ, Kyle, aren't things bad enough! [*Pause.*] Well, you're grounded. Forget the excursion, forget the formal, forget the afterparty, touch footy. Forget your pocket money. School and home, school and home, and that's it.

KYLE: Well, that'll save yas some money, won't it?

>   GEORGE *loses his temper and grabs* KYLE *to shake him out of his petulance.* KYLE *fights back and raises a fist to his father. This is a very ugly exchange which shocks everyone.*

GEORGE: Well, go on, mate, what are you waiting for, go me, come on...

SUZIE: Stop it. Stop it...

>   SUZIE *eventually gets in the way of the two fighting and cops an elbow in the mouth which makes both men stop and stare at her.* GEORGE *moves towards her, but she holds her arm up in the air as if meaning 'don't come near me'.*

>   KYLE *runs off.*

Kyle!

She looks at GEORGE *and expects him to go after their son.*

George.

SCENE SIX: THE TORCH

Twenty minutes later, out in the back paddock of the property, GEORGE *is looking for* KYLE *with a torch.*

GEORGE: Come on, Kyle. You can't stay out here all night. Where are ya? Kyle? [*He stands exasperated in the dark. Pause.*] We copped ya mum a beaudy in the face. [*To himself*] Now everyone'll think I've been beating her. [*Calling out to* KYLE] Come on, mate.

> *He eventually shines the torch on* KYLE *who is huddled up in a corner of the property around some old rusted machinery.*
>
> KYLE *is crying hard and hides his face from the torchlight.* GEORGE *comes over towards him and* KYLE *flinches away from him, curling up further in a tighter ball.* GEORGE *stands away from him. He calms down.*
>
> *Long pause.*

Come on, mate, let's go inside… it's getting cold.

SCENE SEVEN: SCHOOL PART 2

The school principal, MISS PIERCE, *is meeting with* GEORGE *and* KYLE *in her office.*

MISS PIERCE: Look, I understand this is out of character for you, Kyle, you are normally a quiet lad, but he has been absent from a number of classes this term. I'll take it under advisement your thoughts on Mr O'Daniels and I will have a word with him, but that's no excuse for such an extreme act of vandalism, is it? You are so lucky that no great damage was done to the premises and you'd do well to light a candle for Constable Dallas the next time you go to church because she has literally saved your skin. Ten more minutes would have seen you in much deeper trouble and you'd now be hanging over an abyss from which I could not save you.

Now… I won't be pressing any charges. I believe in the power of redemption. Of course you won't be allowed to go on the excursion next week. You'll be suspended from school for twenty days starting today and after that you'll be on thin ice if you want to complete your course requirements for your School Certificate. One more transgression and I can assure you you'll get the wrath of Khan coming down on you. Is that understood, Kyle?

> KYLE *nods his head.*

It's a pity your wife couldn't come down to the school, Mr Petro… I understand things are a little tough at home recently with the property… arh… the way things are… nobody's finding it easy these days, are they?

GEORGE: Like you say, Miss Pierce… this'll be, this is just a one-off thing… thanks so much for that.

> *The meeting with* MISS PIERCE *is over and she ushers them to the door.*

MISS PIERCE: Alright.

> *She shakes hands with* GEORGE.

Think about your future, Kyle.

> KYLE *nods his head as they are led out into the foyer of the school.* MISS PIERCE *exits.* GEORGE *and* KYLE *stand in the foyer silently.* GEORGE *sees a photo on the wall.*

GEORGE: You seen this photo?

> KYLE *begrudgingly looks at it.*

That's me there. With the beard and the mullet. [*He looks at the trophies.*] Thrashed Jindagil by eight goals. Lost the state final to… arh… some school in Albury… Scotch College or something.

KYLE: [*unimpressed with this trip down memory lane*] Losers.

GEORGE: You in any of these photos?

KYLE: No.

GEORGE: Why don't you show some respect?

KYLE: What for?

> GEORGE *walks past him in disgust.*

> *The scene shifts.* SANDIE *approaches* KYLE, *where he was sitting at the start of the chapter.*

SANDIE: You right?

KYLE: Na.

SANDIE: Can't ya come to touch footy no more?

No answer.

I can come to your place and hang out if ya want.

No response.

I'm on the formal committee with Casey, we can have the meetings at your house.

Still no response.

See ya.

She leaves. KYLE *sits bitter and angry with himself and holds his head in his hands.*

END ACT TWO

ACT THREE: SILENCE

SCENE ONE: THE FARM

Eureka. Late afternoon. GEORGE *is herding his livestock through a gate on the family property and feeding them water.* KYLE *watches, not helping.* GEORGE *asks him to fill a tank with water.* KYLE *ignores him and leaves.*

GEORGE *works harder and faster, knowing he has to go into town soon.* SUZIE *calls out to him.*

SUZIE: [*offstage*] George, don't forget to pick up the mail!

SCENE TWO: DRIVE TO TOWN

Music starts. GEORGE *drives into town.* LAURA *is on the side of the road.* GEORGE *pulls over and picks her up.*

LAURA: Thanks, George… one of these days we'll get the second car but 'not at the moment' says Wayne in his usual style. Two years ago we got four hundred dollars per tonne, now they're paying a hundred and fifty. Wayne's had enough. 'I'm pullin' all my grapes out, I'm sick of it,' he says. His father'd turn in his grave if he heard Wayne talkin'. You remember ol' Geoffrey. Big bull of a man. Wayne was never good enough for him. [*Small pause.*] You hear it's flooding in Queensland?

    GEORGE *pulls over and* LAURA *gets out of the car.*

Say hi to Suzie for me. See ya.

SCENE THREE: THE POST OFFICE

GEORGE *goes to his post office box checking his mail.*

VALERIE *walks past. They exchange a quick glance,* GEORGE *smiles but* VALERIE *snarls and walks on.*

GEORGE *opens one letter and reads it. It's the electricity bill.*

STEWART, *the local hardware store owner walks past.*

STEWART: Hey, George. That fencing wire work alright? I'll get some more of those hinges if ya want… they're more expensive now.

GEORGE *smiles and gives the thumbs up as* STEWART *walks away.* GEORGE *opens another letter and it's an insurance bill.* WENDY, *an elderly pensioner, walks past.*

WENDY: More bills? That's all I get in the mail now. They won't get me internet banking, but. They won't get me using that BPAY, either. BPAY, my foot! BPAY, no way!

She walks off as WARREN BLUFF *walks past. The local hairdresser,* FRAN, *walks past.*

FRAN: Hi, George.

GEORGE *smiles another limp hello.*

Pickin' Casey up, are ya? Saw her at the shop, she's a good kid, that girl.

GEORGE *smiles and nods.*

And tell that lovely missus of yours I haven't seen her in too long, that lovely auburn would have faded by now, must be time for a touch-up.

GEORGE *nods again as* FRAN *leaves. He opens another letter and stands reading it as* DOUG, *another farmer, walks past in a hurry.*

DOUG: Hey, Lee Kernaghan, that tractor you sold me? It ain't startin', can ya come over and take a look at her? Give us a ring, you got mi number.

GEORGE *nods, sinks with dispair, shakes his head and goes back to reading his mail, this letter really grabbing his attention.* FATHER SPANIAL *walks past and waves.*

SPANIAL: Hello, George.

He leaves. AMBER *and* ALEX *enter in school uniform.*

AMBER/ALEX: Hello, Mr Petro. We're selling raffle tickets to raise money for King Ciaphas Christian College's new multi-purpose centre.
AMBER: First prize is…
ALEX: … a whipper-snipper.
AMBER: Second prize is…
ALEX: … a set of beach towels.
AMBER: And third prize is…
ALEX: … a trip for six to Broken Hill.
AMBER: Only one dollar a ticket…

ALEX: ... or three dollars for five.

AMBER/ALEX: Would you like to help our school?

>   GEORGE *shakes his head and goes back to reading his mail.*

Thanks, Mr Petro...

>   *They leave.*

... for nothing...

>   GEORGE *returns to reading his mail as* WARREN BLUFF *comes out of his office which is next door to the post office.*

WARREN: Lee Kernaghan... saw ya at the post office a little earlier, rude of me not to say g'day... Warren Bluff... from Warren Bluff Real Estate... You're not in the market for a row of shops in Jindagil, are ya? That's them there. Nice frontage, room galore, parkin' out the back. They been vacant for nearly three years. Owner's'd practically give 'em away, they're so desperate. Mind you, who'd live in Jindagil, eh? More's the point, who'd bloody shop there?

>   WARREN *laughs at his own joke and leaves.* GEORGE *stares stunned at the mystery letter.*

SCENE FOUR: THE PUB

Twenty minutes later in the Royal Hotel, GEORGE *is standing on his own having a beer away from the bar, still reading the same letter.* WEAZEL LOGAN *is talking to* CAROL *the barmaid while she is looking up at 'Wheel of Fortune' on the TV.*

WEAZEL: 'Sale Due To No Work'. That's what it said, what he put on the bottom of the, the, pamphlety thing he'd stuck on the door and on the noticeboard out there, under the list of stuff he had goin'. 'No Work'. No work alright. And I'll tell ya why—

CAROL: [*responding to the TV*] Top dollar, top dollar... Oooooh, 'Bankrupt'.

WEAZEL: ... Asians! That's right. Asians, comin' here in their boatloads and sampans and whatnots, takin' all the jobs, they're takin' 'em, Australian jobs for Australians, no, gone, and what jobs are left are takin' by them Indians and the Afghanis and them other Polynesiani types, trucked over here with their fifteen kids each, big-arse families they got, no wonder Walshy's sellin' up, mate. No wonder. Eh?

CAROL: Yeah, yeah, geez you're a grumpy bum.

WEAZEL: Eh, Carol, you know I'm right, eh. You know I'm right, eh, aren't I? Aren't I?

CAROL: What you are, Weazel, is right ugly, now put your teeth back in, you're puttin' people off their food.

WEAZEL: What people? No-one comes in here no more, this place used to be packed to the rafters on meal time, always, not now, no, where are they? All home watchin' 'Wheel of Fortune' like you are here, waiting for the luck to fall. Or like Walshy, pullin' up stumps and gettin' out. And not just Walshy either. How many other 'For Sale' signs are out there? All up and down the main drag here, how many? Count them.

GEORGE *finishes his beer, waves to* CAROL.

CAROL: See ya, George.

WEAZEL: Mate… this town is dying.

GEORGE *hesitates, thinks, and leaves.*

CAROL: [*to* WEAZEL] Why don't you just shut up?

SCENE FIVE: THE CORNER SHOP

CASEY *is behind the counter talking to a school friend,* CAMERON, *who is in school uniform.*

CASEY: That new girl, right, I said to Sandie that she's either a nerd, a geek, an emo, a slut, a wannabe, a sporty, smoker, popular, non-popular, a reject, conformist, non-conformist, muso, dramatic, druggo, wog, Lebo, Abo, or a religious freak. But whatever she is, she'd better hurry up and make up her mind or she'll be a nothing and there ain't no such thing.

CAMERON: Yeah, right.

CASEY *notices* GEORGE *come in.*

CASEY: Hi, Dad, with ya in a minute…

CAMERON: Hey, Mr Petro.

GEORGE *nods a hello at* CAMERON.

CASEY: Cameron's girlfriend Kelly dropped him. She reckons his sixpack ain't as good as it could be. That's what she said.

CAMERON: Yeah, sucks to be me, eh.

CASEY: Anyways, dude, I gotta go…
CAMERON: Yeah, right. See ya.

>   CAMERON *leaves.*

CASEY: [*to* GEORGE] I'll just get my bag. Car out the front?

>   GEORGE *nods as* CASEY *goes and gets her bag.* MR CHANG *comes out from the back of the shop.*

Mr Chang, my dad's here. See ya next week.
CHANG: Okay, Casey, see you next week. Hello, Mr Petro.

>   GEORGE *nods another hello.*

>   *Music starts.*

SCENE SIX: DRIVE HOME

GEORGE *is driving his daughter* CASEY *home.*

CASEY: Mrs Walsh came in the shop today, heard her talking to Mr Chang, she was saying how their place has already been on the market for ages but no-one'll buy it. Her dad's real old and sick, they gotta go look after him. I was listening on accident. Like, Madison's already been to three high schools already and now they're gonna move to somewhere again, that'll be her fourth school, she's so upset. It's sad seeing people goin' really broke. [*Pause.*] What's for dinner? Hope we're not having mince again.

SCENE SEVEN: HOME

KYLE *is playing a video game in the lounge room as* GEORGE *and* CASEY *enter.*

CASEY: Hi, Mum, what's for dinner?… Oh, excellent… rissoles.

>   CASEY *whacks* KYLE *with her bag as she walks past. They exchange abuse.* CASEY *exits to her room.*

SUZIE: Don't dump your bags there, Casey! Clean up your room please.

>   GEORGE *stands looking at what* KYLE *is playing with a vexed expression.* KYLE *looks almost hypnotised. The sounds are very violent.* SUZIE *goes past* GEORGE *into the kitchen.*

Oh, here he is, the master has returned. Benny got out again. Third time this week. Got his hoof stuck in the driveway grille this time, nearly twisted it right off, poor thing. Stupid. Almost called you to get some medicine for him, then I saw you didn't take your phone. I just put some Dettol on it. Should be right. And, real good news... I heard it on the radio, this area is being put on Level Six water restrictions.

> GEORGE *gives her the mail.*

Anything good? [*At the first bill*] Electricity. That's good. [*At the second bill*] Insurance. That's very good.

> *She stops at the mystery letter and stands reading it, giving* GEORGE *the occasional knowing glance.*

Oh, that's great. That's just terrific. Excellent. What else? [*She folds the letters up.*] You counted how many bales we got left? Go have a count. You're good at Maths. Count 'em.

> *She stands in the kitchin putting the dinner together. She is almost in a state of shock.*

Kyle, get ready for dinner, please, go wash your hands. D'you hear me, Kyle? Kyle!

> KYLE *doesn't answer. The game he is playing gets louder.*

Casey? Come on. Casey!

> CASEY *is in her room talking on her mobile.*

CASEY: [*calling*] Yes, Mum, I'm coming, I'm just talking to Sandie! Be a minute!

> *She goes back to her rave to Sandie as* KYLE*'s game gets louder.*

Yeah, we're having rissoles again... Yeah, more mince. Mince, mince and more mince. That's all we eat now, can't afford any real, like, meat, like, the only meat we eat is mince, I'm sick of it, if I eat any more mince I'll explode. Can I come over to your place to eat...? Mince, mince and more mince. Mince, mince and more mince. Mince, mince and more mince. Mince, mince, mince!

> *By the end of this sequence, the sounds have come to a deafening crescendo.*

GEORGE *can't handle it anymore. He leaves the room and goes out to sit in the car.*

SCENE EIGHT: THE LOWEST EBB

GEORGE *is alone. It is very quiet, only the sounds of night, crickets.*
He gets out of the car, takes his rifle from the cabinet, and sits staring at it. Very long pause.

CASEY: [*calling from inside the house*] Dad!… 'The Footy Show' is on!

> GEORGE *stops his thoughts, thinks twice again, then puts the gun away. He goes back inside the house.*

SCENE NINE: HOME AGAIN

SUZIE *is in the kitchen reading a magazine as* GEORGE *re-enters the house.*

SUZIE: You want a cuppa?

> *Pause.*

GEORGE: Great Grandad bought this place back in 1898. He made that Eureka sign out the front. Now I'm such a useless bastard, I gotta sell it. Can't even feed mi own wife and kids, not like my dad and those before him… Even Grandma kept the farm goin' when Pop fought in the war. 'There's no room for failure,' that's what my dad used to say.

> *He starts crying.* SUZIE *comes over and wipes away his tears. She shakes her head and cries too.*

SUZIE: Is that a no or a yes to a cuppa?

> *Music starts. They wipe away each other's tears. Eventually* SUZIE *leaves,* GEORGE *standing alone looking around at the memorabilia on the walls.*

END ACT THREE

ACT FOUR: BURNT

CASEY: We haven't been on a proper holiday since I was four. My parents have never really travelled. It's harvest time at Christmas, so, like, we can't go anywhere. I remember once when Grandpa was really sick, we were on holidays for a week and then we had to come home and help him out. So my only times away are on school excursions.

SCENE ONE: THE SCHOOL EXCURSION

Students are getting on the bus for the school excursion to Sydney. MR O'DANIELS *is herding everyone on like cattle.*

O'DANIELS: Alright, everyone, on the bus!

    SUZIE *is seeing off* CASEY.

CASEY: But we're staying in a hotel, Mum, I won't need the sleeping bag.

SUZIE: Take it just in case, you never know. I've put in a few extra pairs of undies too.

CASEY: We're only going for two days, Mum.

SUZIE: You can never have enough undies, Casey. And I want you to keep warm, watch what you drink, don't eat anything that doesn't smell right, and ring me when you get there, don't use all your credit on useless calls… and be responsible and don't stray from the group and don't talk to any strangers, if you see any of those bikies, look away, don't look anyone in the eyes, don't you dare go anywhere near Kings Cross…

    GEORGE *and* KYLE *enter.*

GEORGE: See ya, Case.

CASEY: See ya, Dad.

KYLE: Say g'day to the big smoke for me, Sis.

CASEY: See ya later, Wyle D. Kyle-dee.

KYLE: Yeah.

CASEY: Don't bug the hell outta Mum and Dad, and help out a bit, will ya?

KYLE: Yeah.

O'DANIELS: Alright, final call, everyone on... Hello, Kyle, pity you're not coming with us, you'll be sorely missed, mate... I was looking forward to our witty repartee and wily banter.

KYLE: Yeah, I'll miss you too, sir.

O'DANIELS: Alright, everyone on the bus... Come on, Cameron... you can do without your mum for two days.

CAMERON: Sorry, sir...

> CAMERON *gets on the bus.*

O'DANIELS: Move it along there, Oscar, or we'll leave without you...

OSCAR: You wouldn't dare leave without the Os, sir, would ya, plus you need a fall guy in case something goes horribly wrong. Hey, Kyle, s'up? I'll go to one of them strip clubs up the Cross for ya... Stay on line I'll send ya some pics of all those gorgeous girls...

> OSCAR *wags his tongue,* KYLE *gives him the finger.*

> OSCAR, CAMERON *and* CASEY *are all waving goodbye from inside the bus.*

ALL: See yas!

SCENE TWO: CHURCH AND REAL ESTATE

SUZIE *visits* FATHER SPANIAL *in the church while* GEORGE *goes to Warren Bluff Real Estate.*

SUZIE: Excuse me, Father Spanial... I was wondering if I could just have a word...

SPANIAL: Hello, Suzie, nice to see you, come in, come in...

GEORGE: Excuse me, Warren, if I could just have a quick word...

WARREN: Look, it's Lee Kernaghan. Come in, matey, what can I do you for?

GEORGE/SUZIE: I won't take up too much of your time.

WARREN: Not a problem.

SUZIE: I just need to a have a word, arh...

SPANIAL: Sure, sure... come and sit down.

WARREN: You're not here for those bloody Jindagil shops, are ya?

GEORGE: [*smiling*] No...

SPANIAL: Would you like a cup of tea?

SUZIE: No...

WARREN: You want a cuppa or something, bit early for a schooner, isn't it?

GEORGE: No... I'm right...

SUZIE: ... thanks anyway...

WARREN: Well come in, matey, come into my humble office...

GEORGE/SUZIE: I hope I'm not interrupting you...

WARREN: No.

SPANIAL: Of course not.

WARREN: Come in, and take a load off. Watch out for them storage boxes, looks like I'm getting audited, but, actually all this crap is finally goin' to the Pintoon pit. How's the family?

GEORGE: Fine.

> GEORGE *exits the stage as if entering Warren's office.*

SPANIAL: How's the family?

SUZIE: Fine... the kids are both fine...

SPANIAL: I heard about Kyle...

SUZIE: Yes...

SPANIAL: Kids will be kids... at least nothing...

SUZIE: ... was... too badly damaged, yes...

SPANIAL: Yes.

> *Pause.*

SUZIE: Um... no, arh... the kids are fine, they do what they do, they don't help that much, sure they help a little, that's why God created the cattle prod... but they care more for arh... it's iPods and mobiles and computer games and ghds and... arh... it's all...

> *Small pause as* SUZIE *tries to control herself.*

SPANIAL: Sorry, what's a ghd?

SUZIE: A... a sort of... whiz-bang hair straightener thing.

SPANIAL: Sure. Sorry. Continue.

SUZIE: George... After the twins were born I wasn't well enough to drive, so I was totally reliant on George. He couldn't stop farming just to ferry me around the countryside. Now, I'm racing around, here and there... arh...

> SPANIAL's *mobile phone rings. He rises out of his chair to answer it and leaves* SUZIE *hanging in mid-thought.*

SPANIAL: Excuse me I have to answer this… Hello?

> WARREN *and* GEORGE *re-enter,* WARREN *is on his mobile phone.*

WARREN: Hello, Charlie? Matey, it's Warren Bluff, listen I got another auction for ya, out near Gilpendry, property called Eureka, we got an auction date in four weeks' time, the fifteenth… are you available is the big question? [*To* GEORGE] He's the best. Checking his diary. Mate, Kenny Walsh has been trying to sell his farm for ages but no-one'll buy a farm that ain't maintained and operating. Yours is. Ya miles ahead… [*Back to the phone*] Yes, mate. We're on?… Excellent… Alrighty, I'll send ya through all the details… You too, mate, yes… No worries. [*He hangs up.*] Sorted. How 'bout I come over this arvo, give it a once over and we'll see what we can do for ya. Yeah?

GEORGE: Yeah.

> *They shake hands.*

WARREN: [*trying to make* GEORGE *feel better*] Mate, a lot of blokes are finding it tough… When all's said and done, there's only so much a man can bash his head against a brick wall, eh? And who wants to sit around on the front porch and wait for the food parcel to arrive? No, I think you're doin' the right thing. You wait and see, in a month's time you'll have a big load off your mind. Yeah?

GEORGE: Yeah.

> WARREN *moves away from* GEORGE *as if back into the agency.* GEORGE *stands a little shell-shocked,* FATHER SPANIAL *re-enters with* SUZIE.

SPANIAL: Well, that's a load off my mind, that's the Rotary board confirming the lad from the United Arab Emirates. Graham Landfill's checked his diary and he's keen to take him in, so that's sorted. What a time? I'm so sorry, Suzie, you were saying?

SUZIE: [*after a pause, smiling but frosty*] I'm not sure what I was saying Father, I just know that the future doesn't look very… happy… and… if ever there was a time when the clouds above would part and the Good Lord would smile down upon us and shower us with a few weeks of rain, it's right now.

SCENE THREE: POWERHOUSE MUSEUM

Up high on the top level of the Sydney Powerhouse Museum, MR O'DANIELS *is taking his Year Ten excursion group on a guided tour.*

O'DANIELS: And from up on this level one feels like the Good Lord himself up in the clouds, looking down on some of the most amazing advancements in travel over the past one hundred years, from the steam engine, to the Apollo spaceship suspended from the ceiling... absolutely amazing... Alright, move it along there, Angus, don't break the exhibits, son.

> CAMERON *and* CASEY *drift into the* O'DANIELS *zone and start looking down on the people at the museum.*

CAMERON: Look, there's some posh rich Sydney School, check them out. Look at what that girl's wearing, my God.

CASEY: She thinks she's so hot, but actually, she's so not. Oooooo.

O'DANIELS: Impressed with the view, Casey?

CASEY: Very impressed, sir, this place is insanely awesome.

O'DANIELS: And what have you enjoyed so far, Cameron?

CAMERON: Everything, sir, it's all great, especially all those gorgeous girls down there. I think I'll accidentally miss the bus home so I can stay here and live in Sydney if that's okay with you.

O'DANIELS: I think that's fine, Cameron, I might give Oscar the same option, Oscar?

> OSCAR *comes on.*

OSCAR: Hey sir, when are we goin' up the Cross? [*Seeing the Sydney girls that* CAMERON *is looking at*] Hey, check out those sexy Sydney girls in the purple uniforms... [*He calls out to them.*] G'day, darlin', my name's Oscar, Oscar the Horse, come up here and I'll show ya why. [*Exiting*] Hey, Dougy... I think I'm in love...

CAMERON: I can see myself living in Sydney.

CASEY: Yeah?

CAMERON: Yeah. I reckon. Go to uni. Get a job in one of those highrise buildings. Marry one of those hotties. Live in a penthouse apartment. Drive a Porsche. Sweet as. You?

CASEY: Nar. Too noisy. Too crowded. I dunno. It's a big change.

CAMERON: Yeah, huge. That's my whole point.

Small pause.

CASEY: S'pose I could get used to it.

SCENE FOUR: CHANGE

A range of characters across town discuss change. ALFIE SHRAPNEL *and* MRS SNODGRASS *are shopping in Capelands' Hardware.*

ALFIE: All they know is how to swan around in their highrise buildings and penthouse apartments and drive their Porsches and meanwhile the wool industry carks it and the Yanks buy out GrainCorp, and we're fed crap about 'fossil fuel rejuvenation', like that bloke who sold Walshy the idea of growing rice a few years ago, I told him, 'Leave the rice to the Chinese,' but did he listen to me?

> STEWART CAPELAND *enters carrying a bag of fertiliser.*

STEWART: I don't think anyone listens to you, Alfie.

ALFIE: That's my whole point. You ask any of us old-timers round here, me—Weazel Logan, the Snodgrasses—does anyone in the cities really think twice about where their milk and butter and bread and sausages come from? They bloody well will when they wake up tomorrow and find it costs them double.

STEWART: But they won't 'cause it's already being imported from China or Romania or somewhere else at half the cost?

ALFIE: Well, I can't get used to that.

> *Meanwhile, at the hairdresser's,* FRAN WHIPPLE *enters with hair dye. She is doing* BRONWYN BOWTELL's *hair.*

FRAN: Yes, it is a big change, Bronwyn, but I think that's the whole point, I think you'll find people will get used to it very quickly.

BRONWYN: I have seen a lot of changes in my time, Fran, but if I can't water my garden every morning and every afternoon then the govern-ment can make the Murray River flow backwards for all I care... I want my garden back!

> *At the police station,* RANJIT SINGH *is talking to* SENIOR CONSTABLE DALLAS.

SINGH: But that is entirely my point, Constable Dallas, if I can afford to offer some of the local farmers here a job at a reasonable cost then why should I be branded some kind of opportunist. Tell me, why?

DALLAS: Yeah, but do you know who threw the egg at you, Mr Singh?

SINGH: The egg is not the issue, it is the principle, the world is changing and people will have to get used to that.

Back at the hairdresser's, BRONWYN *is talking to* MAGGIE COLLINGWOOD.

BRONWYN: It's very hard to get used to it.

MAGGIE: I don't like it one bit either but what can I do? I'm comfortable staying the woman that I am. And Barry doesn't complain... I know how to keep a marriage together... three times a week.

They all laugh out loud.

FRAN: Well, I don't know if you've heard yet, girls, but the big news, you are not going to believe it—

BRONWYN: I've heard about that Indian fellow being egged, and it wasn't me.

The girls giggle.

FRAN: No, no, no... the big news is... the Petros are selling Eureka.

BRONWYN/MAGGIE: What?!

FRAN: Yep. The Petros are selling up.

SCENE FIVE: FAMILY BUSINESS

The bus for the excursion arrives back at the school. It's early evening. GEORGE *waits.* CAMERON *gets off the bus. He's very sick and tired.*

CAMERON: Hey, Mr Petro. Casey's on her way, she's just getting her bag. I think I ate too many Twisties. See ya. Hey, Mum...

CAMERON *moves away as* CASEY *gets off the bus.*

CASEY: Hey, Dad. See ya, Cameron.

CAMERON: Yeah...

CASEY: [*to* GEORGE] Where's Mum?

GEORGE: Home. How was it?

CASEY: Oh yeah, it was so awesome... I didn't sleep one bit, I mean, at all... everyone was so excited the whole time we were there... the hotel was so nice... no-one could like shut up, I swear to God I could sleep for five whole days... the museum, my God, they had all these, like, exhibitions and that, like, and we saw the chick from

'McLeod's Daughters', I thought that program was shot in Adelaide somewhere but she lives in Sydney, some girls went over to talk to her but I was too shy… and the Powerhouse Museum, like…

The scene shifts to home.

GEORGE: We're home.

CASEY: Hi, Mum.

SUZIE: Hello, Casey… welcome home… you hungry? You want something to eat? I'll bet you're tired…

CASEY: No, yeah, sorta, we ate at this truckstop, I'm full… I swear to God I could sleep for five whole days, but, Mum, shoulda seen it, it was awesome… the museum, my God, they had all these, like, exhibitions and that, like, and we saw the chick from 'McLeod's Daughters', I thought that program was shot in Adelaide somewhere but she lives in Sydney, some girls went over to talk to her but I was too shy… and her hair was super straight!

GEORGE: Kyle?

KYLE: Yeah?

GEORGE: Come here.

KYLE: Hey, Case. How's the big smoke?

CASEY: Awesome, we saw the chick from 'McLeod's Daughters', I thought that program was shot in Adelaide somewhere but she lives in Sydney…

GEORGE: We thought we'd wait till you got back from your trip to tell yas both what's goin' on.

Small pause. KYLE *starts to play his video game.* CASEY's *mobile goes off.*

CASEY: That'll be Sandie, just a sec.

GEORGE: [*very loud*] Turn it off!

CASEY *turns her phone off.* KYLE *turns off his game. They both stare at* GEORGE.

We're sellin' the farm. [*Pause.*] Every year when that big cheque arrives for the crop your mother and me spend it straight away to make sure we get next year's crop. This year, there won't be one. I borrowed too much and… now the bank… [*Small pause.*] Auction's in four weeks' time. [*Smaller pause.*] Sell the place, go somewhere

where I can get a job. Ya mother too. Youse'll finish Year Ten, and do Years Eleven and Twelve at another school.

KYLE and CASEY are shocked by the news. KYLE gets up and leaves.

Kyle?

A very uncomfortable pause.

CASEY: Where'll we go?

Small pause.

GEORGE: I don't know.

Pause. CASEY goes to her room. The two parents stand looking at each other.

SCENE SIX: FOR SALE

Flies are buzzing and the occasional sheep sounds are heard. WARREN BLUFF brings on a very large 'For Sale' sign and puts it out the front of the Eureka property. CHARLIE SELMAN enters with two large animal skulls.

CHARLIE: My old mate, Warren Bluff!

WARREN: G'day, Charlie... brought a few friends, did ya?

CHARLIE: I found stacks of these all along the back fence, not a good look, smells of death around here.

WARREN: Not as big as Walshy's either.

Benny barks at CHARLIE.

CHARLIE: Piss off, ya mangy lookin' mongrel bitch...

SUZIE enters.

SUZIE: Benny! Down, boy.

WARREN: Here she is, the lady of the house, *Introducing* Suzie Petro, Charlie Selman. Charlie, Suzie.

CHARLIE: Lovely to meet you, Suzie. Nice dog. Benny, is it?

WARREN: Charlie'll be running the show next Saturday...

CHARLIE: I found a whole heap of these up the back paddock... I remember I did a sale out near Scone once and this fella from Canberra showed up and bought a half dozen of these at fifty dollars a pop... So you never know what things are worth...

SUZIE: They scare off the crows.

CHARLIE: I'll bet they do.

WARREN: Charlie can sell sand to the Arabs.

CHARLIE: I saw your good husband, he's doin' a bit of tractor work down the back paddock there, and he told me to come and ask you the same question I asked him… Now there's a few ways we can go about this: we can sell the lot all in one big go, lock, stock and barrel, highest bidder wins, no questions asked, it can be all over in a matter of seconds; or, you can sell it in chunks, the property, the house, the livestock, the machinery, or each individual item… the mower, the shovel, the spade, the crockery, the spoons. In fact, Warren and I we did a place in Gindigil not that long ago and the owner was well pleased with the result, he had no idea how much he could make for that junky old china of his… plus, there's always those second-hand vultures from Sydney or Melbourne who come snoopin' round for a bargain, the idea is to rip them off before they rip off the punters from Toorak or Rose Bay. So, what's it to be… the lot… chunks… or bits and pieces?

SCENE SEVEN: THE AUCTION

Eureka is open for inspection before the auction. STEWART *enters and approaches* SUZIE.

STEWART: G'day, Suzie. Howzitgoin', eh?

SUZIE: G'day, Stewart.

    GRAHAM *enters.*

GRAHAM: Suzie, anything the Rotarians can do, you let me know!

SUZIE: Thanks, Graham.

    BRONWYN *enters.*

BRONWYN: Suzie love. Don't worry about the fundraiser, we've got it covered.

SUZIE: Thanks, Bronwyn.

    MILES *enters.*

MILES: Oh, Suzie, I had to see this to believe it.

    DOUG *enters.*

DOUG: It's come to this, has it?

ALFIE *enters.*

ALFIE: It's a crying shame is what it is.

MR CHANG *enters.*

CHANG: Hello, Mrs Petro. I'm so sorry. You know Casey can still keep her job, whatever happens.
SUZIE: Thanks, Mr Chang.

COLIN KALM *enters with baby.*

COLIN: Has it started yet?

WEAZEL *enters.*

WEAZEL: Suzie… what can I say? Jesus. [*He moves over to* GEORGE.] George, Jesus, mate… what can I say?

LAURA *enters.*

LAURA: Wayne couldn't make it, said to say g'day.

FATHER SPANIAL *enters.*

SPANIAL: I don't think we've been formally introduced, George, I'm Father Spanial, and if there's anything I can do to help, please don't hesitate to drop by.

FRAN *enters.*

FRAN: Hello, George, how you keeping up, mate? Hello, Father.
SPANIAL: Hello, Fran.
FRAN: What a crowd? Hello, Suzie.

WARREN *enters.*

WARREN: [*to* GEORGE] Chin up, mate, we're about ready to start.

WENDY *enters.*

WENDY: George, if you need anything, something for the kids…
GEORGE: Thanks, Mrs Snodgrass.
WENDY: Don't be too proud to ask.

KYLE *comes up close to his dad and looks at all the people.*

GEORGE: Well, you got what you wanted, didn't ya?

GEORGE *moves away.* CASEY *enters and talks to her brother.*

CASEY: Heaps a people.

KYLE: Vultures.

> SINGH *enters.*

SINGH: Excuse me, I am looking for Mr George Petro, can you tell me where I can find him please?

CASEY: The one in the hat. Over there.

SINGH: He looks like Lee Kernaghan. Thank you. [*Exiting*] Excuse me, Mr Petro, my name is Ranjit Singh…

> SINGH *exits.* KYLE *leaves.* CAMERON *enters.*

CAMERON: Hey, Casey.

CASEY: Hi, Cameron. Did ya mum give you a lift out?

CAMERON: Nar, I walked.

CASEY: From your place?

CAMERON: Yeah. Hope youse don't sell the farm. Then youse can stay.

> CHARLIE SELMAN *enters quickly.*

CHARLIE: Alrighty, let's get this turkey gobbling. [*To* CAMERON] You, mate, piss off.

> CAMERON *leaves.*

> *Sound effects begin and the mood suddenly gets very strange.*

[*To* CASEY] You… you can stay, and watch your worst nightmare…

> CASEY *reels in horror as* CHARLIE SELMAN *takes the stand, holding up the two large animal skulls, using them as pointers.*

Ladies and gentlemen, welcome. This property, you all know it well, it's going for a bargain, that's right, Eureka… all twelve hundred and fifty hectares, complete with homestead, shed, garage, livestock and orchard. This is a potential goldmine for anyone who wants to turn a graveyard into a garden!

Starting price: nine hundred. Who wants to give me nine hundred? Nine hundred over there. Eight hundred and fifty? That's lower, but I'll take it, eight hundred and fifty it is, eight fifty, eight hundred. Six ninety-five. Ooo, that's a sharp plummet, six ninety-five, six twenty. Five twenty. Four hundred. It's going down down down faster faster faster, four hundred is the bid, we have four hundred, who'll do better than four hundred? Four hundred… three hundred. Three hundred now the bid, do I hear anything below three hundred? Two twenty. That's more like it. Two twenty. One twenty. One ten—that's about as long as this family has been here—one ten, sixty-five! Only sixty-five. Sixty-five the bid, anything lower than sixty-five? Twenty-five? Twenty-five, only twenty-five… two. Two is the bid. I'll take two. Two dollars the bid. Two dollars for this slice of farming failure. Two dollars. Two dollars. Two dollars for the house, the shed, the property, the livestock and the whole family history! Two dollars the bid. Going once at two dollars for Eureka. Ten cents. Ten cents. That's all it's worth. That's what this family has toiled its heart out for over a hundred years. Ten cents, ladies and gentlemen… going once, going twice…

CASEY: Stop! Stop it…

All stop. Silence.

CHARLIE SELMAN *leaps off his podium and stands behind* CASEY *holding the animal skulls between her head. He looks up menacingly at the crowd, highlighting* CASEY*'s nightmare image.*

CHARLIE: No sale!

He leaves, taking the 'For Sale' sign with him.

SCENE EIGHT: SECOND THOUGHTS

Outside school at the end of the day. CASEY *and* KYLE *stand waiting for their lift home.*

CASEY: Where do ya reckon we'll go?
KYLE: Last night I thought about running away. Was gonna hitch a ride with some truckie dude.
CASEY: Where would ya go?
KYLE: Broome.
CASEY: Why Broome?
KYLE: 'Cause it's the furthest away from here.
CASEY: Is that 'cause ya got a crush on Sandie and you haven't asked her to the formal yet?
KYLE: Who told ya that?
CASEY: Derrr. [*Small pause.*] Here she is.
KYLE: Bags the front.

SUZIE *arrives in the car to pick them up.*

SUZIE: Sorry I'm late. Just had to see the Principal for a minute.

KYLE: What'd I do now?

SUZIE: Oh, we had a good chat about you, Kyle.

KYLE: I'll bet ya did.

SUZIE: And you too, Casey?

KYLE: Where's Dad?

SUZIE: We're pickin' him up from in town. [*Small pause.*] The big question I have for you, mister… when are you gonna ask Sandie to the formal?

KYLE: What?

SUZIE: There he is.

GEORGE *is waiting on the side of the road. The car pulls over.*

GEORGE: [*to* KYLE, *pointing to the back seat*] In the back.

KYLE *begrudgingly gets out and gets in the back and sits next to* CASEY. GEORGE *sits in the front passenger seat.*

SUZIE: How'd you go?

GEORGE: How'd you go?

SUZIE: I asked you first.

GEORGE: Ladies first.

SUZIE: No way, I'm driving.

GEORGE: No, no… come on… you're the pretty one, you have to answer first.

SUZIE: No way.

KYLE: What are yas talking about?

GEORGE: Have you asked Sandie to the formal yet?

KYLE: What's all this crap about Sandie, thought we weren't goin'. I'm grounded anyway. Good one, Sis. What are yas on about?

SUZIE: So you got it?

GEORGE: Looks like it. You?

KYLE: Got what? What's goin' on?

GEORGE: I offered my services to Mr Ranjit Singh to help him out on his property, plus… I sold him half our stock.

SUZIE: [*very surprised, slamming on the brakes*] What?

GEORGE: He's gonna give us a big, fat, up-front fee plus pay me by the hour to run his farm.

SUZIE: For how long?

GEORGE: Just for this next harvest and then see what happens.

SUZIE: Will that cover...?

GEORGE: No... won't cover all the debts... but... arh... it's enough. Enough to tell Warren Bluff to shove it.

SUZIE: [*slightly overwhelmed*] Oh... that's...

> *They are both out of words. Pause.*

GEORGE: And you? What'd Miss Pierce say?

SUZIE: As of next week I start working part-time at the school.

GEORGE: In the office?

SUZIE: Not exactly. [*She sees the supermarket.*] I've just got to go in there for a second.

GEORGE: You gonna be long?

SUZIE: Ten minutes. Fifteen.

GEORGE: I'll duck in for a quick schooner. You kids wait here.

> SUZIE *and* GEORGE *leave the car.* KYLE *and* CASEY *sit waiting.*

KYLE: Who's been talking about Sandie, you traitor?

CASEY: You're a dickhead.

> *The scene shifts to the supermarket check-out with* MIRIANA *beeping through* RANJIT SINGH*'s groceries.* SUZIE *waits in line behind him.*

MIRIANA: That's fifty-four twenty-five, thank you.

SINGH: Fifty...?

MIRIANA: Fifty-four twenty-five. Cash or credit?

SINGH: Yes, cash, thank you very, very much.

MIRIANA: FlyBuys?

SINGH: No thank you.

MIRIANA: Thank you very much. Have a nice day.

SINGH: And you have a glorious day, my girl.

> *He leaves.* SUZIE *comes up to* MIRIANA.

SUZIE: Just the Tim Tams thanks.

> MIRIANA *beeps it through.*

SCENE NINE: BURNT

The Royal Hotel. GEORGE *is drinking a beer with* WEAZEL. CAROL *is behind the bar.*

WEAZEL: It rained in '83. I think Bob Hawke made it rain, didn't he? We all celebrated, but the months leading into the summer of '85 were alarmingly dry. We were all nervous, we had no stock because of the drought, there was feed everywhere as high as the fence, fit to burn. There were fires around the whole state. We got burnt out on Australia Day, 1985. Twenty-five farms were affected. We lost about a third of our place, six hundred sheep. There were other places that were totally burnt out. It was hellish… Your father found it particularly hard, but you didn't know that, did ya?

GEORGE *remembers the fire.*

Fires, they're quick, deadly, devastating, tragic… good news footage. But drought's different. It's slow, painful and seemingly endless. Death is all around you. Closes in on ya like the slow-motion jaws of an animal trap.

CAROL: Oh, would ya listen to the bush poet… Mr Weazel Logan, ladies and gentlemen, Gilpendry's own Henry Lawson?

WEAZEL: Go ahead, Carol, take the piss, but there'll be hard times ahead. You wait and see. [*He finishes his schooner and goes to leave.*] See yas later.

GEORGE: Yeah, I guess you will.

Music starts.

EPILOGUE

Eureka. GEORGE *and* CASEY *are feeding the animals.*

CASEY: It's been to leave or not to leave, this past year now.

We got no more food, for the… no bales, like, I've grown up on the farm, so's mi Mum and Dad, that's what we do, we have to get the fruit picked, the sheep shorn, my dad doesn't have a trade up his sleeve, so he'll just, like, work for whoever, keep our place goin… we'll just keep goin' till we can't.

Dad was doing his will the other day, he asked me what to leave us in their will, and we said don't leave us the farm.

Dad said, 'Promise me you'll never sell Eureka'.

I promised.

GEORGE *stands looking up at the sky, hoping for rain.*

Music ends.

THE END

From left: Günther Henne as Will, Michael Meyer as iBoy, Susanne Schyns as Xenia and Kim Pfeiffer as Leah in the 2010 Theaterhaus Frankfurt production of TABU (TABOO) directed by Tom Lycos. (Photo: Katrin Schander)

TABOO

WRITERS' NOTE:
A SPECIAL RELATIONSHIP

In 2000, Sydney Theatre Company presented Zeal Theatre's *The Stones* for a two-week season at the Wharf Theatre as part of the STC Ed program. Over the next few years, Zeal would perform *Side Effects*, *A Secret Place* and a return season of *The Stones* in the same venue. A special relationship between the two companies was steadily developing. The artistic director of STC at that time, Robyn Nevin, was keen to strengthen the links between our two companies and support our work and so commissioned us to write a new play, and in 2006 we wrote *Gronks*. The success of *Gronks* lead to a second and third STC commission and in 2007 we wrote *Australia v South Africa* and *Taboo*.

We wanted to write a play which was a warning to young people who may put themselves in vulnerable situations through internet dating. We also wanted to celebrate the struggles of a young girl who, after being raped by a number of men, had the courage to go to the police and was determined to see justice through the courts. That girl's name is Tegan Wagner. Her story is well documented in numerous books, articles and media reports. She was a hero to us and her story mixed with the explosion of internet dating stories we were gathering were the inspiration points for *Taboo*.

Addressing powerful and complex social issues for young people in a safe and respectful manner is at the core or why we do what we do as a theatre company. Most of Zeal Theatre's work has been primarily targeted at high school audiences and most of the productions have been researched and developed with the assistance of young people through workshops and meetings we conduct with schools who continue regular contact with us. This process was undoubtedly of the utmost importance for the creation of *Taboo*. Numerous students from numerous schools were involved in the development of the script and we would like to thank them all for their openness and honesty.

Taboo has been translated and performed in Germany by Theaterhaus Frankfurt and in Norway by Teater Grimsborken, both productions directed by Tom Lycos. We have maintained a special relationship with these and other European companies who, since 2000, have produced versions of our plays: Arad Goch Theatre in Wales, MUZtheater in The Netherlands, Kolibri Theater in Hungary, Teatret Neo in Denmark and the National Theatre in England.

Tom Lycos and Stefo Nantsou
December 2010

FIRST PRODUCTION

Taboo was originally commissioned by Sydney Theatre Company and was first performed on 2 December 2007 at Canley Vale High School, Sydney, with the following cast:

XENIA	Lindy Sardelic
LEAH / YOLANDA / MC	Sandy Greenwood
CHAD / NICK / iBoy / FILM BUFF KID 1	Tom Lycos
MR PITCHKA / TRAIN PERVE / DARRYL / ZUBIN / MOHAMMED / WILL / FILM BUFF KID 2	Stefo Nantsou

Directed by Tom Lycos and Stefo Nantsou

CHARACTERS

MR PITCHKA, teacher

LEAH, 14

XENIA, 14

CHAD, Leah's father

DARRYL, Chad's friend

YOLANDA, Xenia's mother

ZUBIN, Xenia's father

NICK, 19, Xenia's brother

MOHAMMED, Nick's friend

iBoy, Leah's computer date

WILL, iBoy's friend

TRAIN PERVE

FILM BUFF KID 1, 12

FILM BUFF KID 2, 12

OXFORD TAVERN MC

sign in, log on, i post my pictures all over your screen
every night, i don't sleep, i'm in love with the secrets we keep

you're watching me, i'm sending my message to you

friday night, lies and lies, fake the truth for the millionth time
nobody knows, where i'm goin', i'm gonna touch you for the very
first time

i'm watching you, you're sending a message to me
you're watching me, i'm watching you, it's taboo

timeless love, any place, webcam sex on cyberspace
but tonight, for real, i'm in a danger that i like to feel

you're touching me, i'm touching you, it's taboo
you're dating me, i'm dating you, it's taboo
you're loving me, i'm loving you, it's taboo

SCENE ONE: SCHOOL

2.55 p.m. A Year Nine health class at St Almighty Girls College.

MR PITCHKA: The penis, now fully erect, enters the vagina. At the point
of ejaculation, the penis shoots zillions of tiny sperm deep up inside
the vagina, the sperm swimming their way up to the ovaries and it
only takes one of those zillion sperms to fertilise the female egg, and
causing conception.

LEAH: Causing what, sir?

MR PITCHKA: Conception, Leah. The girl gets pregnant. Not always, of
course, but the odds vary from individual to individual. Skye might
become pregnant the first time she has sex but poor Cloud may
never become pregnant no matter how many times she has sex. So
it is always a good idea, girls, to have safe sexual practices if you
want to avoid pregnancy… and also using a condom can protect
you from some nasty sexually transmitted infections.

LEAH: Oooooo.

MR PITCHKA: Thank you, Leah. Alright, now you've already split into pairs, that's good, now one of you hold the penis upright, and the other girl will open the condom packet, take out the condom, give it a little stretch, not too hard, Harrissa, that's good, don't use your teeth opening the condom packet, Xenia, you don't want to put a hole in the condom, that's not a very good idea, now place the condom over the end of the plastic penis and then roll it on. That's very good, Skye, stop giggling, thanks, Cloud, hold it firmly or she won't be able to get it on. Much better.

XENIA: He must get so embarrassed teaching all this stuff to girls.

LEAH: He loves it, look at him.

MR PITCHKA: Not so frenzied, Verena, nice and calm.

XENIA: Did you pinch all those condoms?

LEAH: Yeah, I took five.

XENIA: Five?

LEAH: Four for me, one for you, and you can have the fluoro one so you know where to put it.

XENIA: Yeah, great.

> LEAH's *mobile phone buzzes, she receives a text.*

MR PITCHKA: Now, remove the condom, tie it all up nicely in a little knot, you don't want spillage all over you, girls, and dispose of it carefully as I demonstrated earlier. That's great, Jemma, looks like you've done this before.

LEAH: Sweet. We're on for tonight.

XENIA: What's his name again?

LEAH: Mine or yours?

XENIA: The guy, that guy, yours.

LEAH: iBoy.

XENIA: 'iBoy'? What's his real name?

LEAH: Dunno.

XENIA: Probably Dwayne… or Derrick.

LEAH: iBoy is a cool name.

XENIA: Yeah, right.

MR PITCHKA: Now give your penis to your partner and you have a go.

LEAH: Did ya like the picture I downloaded of his friend?

XENIA: Yeah… he's pretty cute, what's his name again?

LEAH: His name's Will. God, Xenia. You forget everything.

XENIA: Is that his real name or his computer name?

LEAH: 'Computer name', you're so lame.

MR PITCHKA: Just give it to her, Skye, thank you.

XENIA: Well, at least Will is better than 'iBoy', what sort of stupid name is that anyway? 'Hey, baby, give us a kiss, my name's iBoy.'

LEAH: Shut up. He's nice.

MR PITCHKA: What are you two girls talking about?

LEAH/XENIA: Nothing, Mr Pitchka.

> *Music starts.*

MR PITCHKA: Alright, there's the bell, bring those penises back to me, girls, and we'll pick this up again on Monday.

SCENE TWO: AFTER SCHOOL

3.37 p.m. LEAH *and* XENIA *are on a train. A* MAN *is behind them, overhearing their conversation.*

TRAIN ANNOUNCER: [*voice*] Doors closing, please stand clear.

LEAH: You'll never guess what I did, but.

XENIA: What?

LEAH: I shouldn't tell you this.

XENIA: Well, you've said it now so tell me.

LEAH: I dared iBoy to strip for me on his iCam.

XENIA: Oh my God… Did he?

LEAH: Yeah, he did, and what a hot body, then he asked me to take my top off.

XENIA: Leah… You didn't, did you?

LEAH: Yeah, I did. He said I was the hottest girl he's ever seen, then I got scared and turned the computer off… I think I'm gonna marry him.

XENIA: Are you nuts, you hardly know the guy.

LEAH: We've been talking on the computer for three months. I think I know him enough to know he's my soul mate.

XENIA: Soul mate, yeah, right. You haven't shown your boobs to Will too, have you?

LEAH: I'm not a slut. Besides, Will's yours, you can show him your boobs tonight.

XENIA: Yeah, right.

> XENIA *and* LEAH *notices the* MAN *perving on them.*

LEAH: Having a good perve, are ya, mate?

XENIA: Leah!

The MAN *is embarrassed and looks away.*

LEAH: I haven't talked to Will as much as iBoy, but he seems nice, a bit shy. Perfect for you.

XENIA: Oh my God, I'm so nervous.

LEAH: Stop worrying about it.

XENIA: It's alright for you.

TRAIN ANNOUNCER: [*voice*] Next stop Cockburn, Cockburn next stop.

XENIA: I told my mum and dad we were going to see *The Sound of Music 2*, that's if your parents ask.

LEAH: It's just Dad at home tonight. He's cool. He won't mind. I'll tell him we're seeing *Halloween 9*.

XENIA: *Sound of Music 2.*

LEAH: Whatever.

The train stops. They get off the train and head to Leah's house.

LEAH: Now don't forget, let me do all the talking, okay?

XENIA: Okay.

LEAH: Okay.

SCENE THREE: LEAH'S HOUSE

4.14 p.m. LEAH*'s father,* CHAD, *is on a computer. His friend* DARRYL *is looking over his shoulder at the screen. The girls arrive home.*

LEAH: Hi, Dad.

CHAD: Hello.

XENIA: Hi, Mr Sedar.

CHAD: I told you to call me Chad, Xenia?

XENIA: Alright, Mr Sedar.

LEAH: Hi, Darrooole.

DARRYL: Hi, Leayahrrr.

LEAH: Darryl Xenia, Xenia Darryl.

DARRYL: Hi.

XENIA: Hi.

LEAH: Xenia's staying here tonight, Dad. I already told Mum about it, she said it was okay as long as I cleaned my room which I already did. We're going to the movies.

CHAD: Oh yeah… what are you gonna see?

LEAH: *Mission Impossible 4.*

CHAD: That's for fifteen and over, youse girls are only fourteen. Too young.

LEAH: Oh yeah, right, as if Tom Cruise'll mess up our minds.

CHAD: He messed up Nicole's mind. He's gay that guy, it's obvious.

LEAH: You're so random, Dad.

> LEAH *moves off to her room,* XENIA*'s attention gets caught on what the men are looking at on computer.*

CHAD: What about this one?

DARRYL: She's good.

CHAD: What do you think of this girl, Xenia?

XENIA: Is she a model or something?

CHAD: No, we're trying to find a nice girl for Darryl here.

XENIA: Like, Lavalife, one of those singles dating things?

DARRYL: Yeah… thought I'd give it go. See what happens.

XENIA: Where's your photo?

DARRYL: Show her mine.

CHAD: Here's the dashing Darryl. There he is.

DARRYL: Don't look too old, do I?

XENIA: No.

LEAH: Xenia, stop talking to my dad. Dad, stop boring my friends.

XENIA: Right-oh…

> XENIA *goes to Leah's room.*

CHAD: What about this one?

DARRYL: She's good.

LEAH: I gotta see if I got any messages. I asked him not to text me in case Sky Channel got hold of my phone. She's such an 'Ano' bitch. He didn't text you, did he?

XENIA: Who?

LEAH: iBoy, God Xenia?

XENIA: Why would he do that?

LEAH: 'Cause I gave him your number in case my battery was dead.

XENIA: Oh my God.

CHAD: What about this one?

DARRYL: She's good.

LEAH: What are you gonna wear?

XENIA: I was gonna wear my full-length veil.

LEAH: Yeah, that's a real turn-on… [*She reads her message on the phone.*] Here he is… my man, yes, 'Seven thirty outside Fox, Will's picking us up in his car'. Shweet. [*She types a return message.*] 'See you then, can't wait, I'm all wet thinking about it.'

XENIA: You can't write that.

LEAH: Why not? Right-oh, right-oh… [*She erases that part of the message.*] 'Can't wait to see you in the flesh.' There. How's that. Send.

XENIA: Oh my God.

CHAD: What about this one?

LEAH: Wanna see a photo of him with his shirt off?

DARRYL: Nice figure.

LEAH: Hot body, eh.

XENIA: Least he hasn't got a hairy back.

LEAH: Ooooo.

CHAD: Least she hasn't got a hairy face.

DARRYL: Ooo.

LEAH: And here's one of Will, with his shirt on.

XENIA: Sweet. God, he looks real old, nineteen at least.

LEAH: I think he's twenty. iBoy's twenty.

XENIA: Twenty, oh my God. Mum'll kill me.

LEAH: She won't find out. Can I borrow your black skirt? You can have my grey one.

XENIA: I'm not wearing grey.

LEAH: Let's go.

DARRYL: I'll get us a couple of beers.

> DARRYL *leaves.*

LEAH: Dad, we're going over to Xenia's to get ready. Can I have some money?

CHAD: How youse getting to the movies?

LEAH: Xenia's dad is giving us a lift.

CHAD: Sure?

LEAH: Yeah.

> *The girls exchange a glance,* XENIA *shaking her head.* LEAH *motions that it's okay.* CHAD *gives her money.*

CHAD: Now that you've fleeced me, I'll be at the shop for a couple of hours this arvo, but I'll be home by ten if you need me.

LEAH: Thanks.

CHAD: Text me.

LEAH/XENIA: We'll be right.

Music starts.

SCENE FOUR: XENIA'S HOUSE

6.26 p.m. Xenia's home. YOLANDA *is in the kitchen serving dinner on the table.* NICK *is in the garage working on his car, revving the motor loudly.* XENIA *is trying to get* NICK's *attention but he is distracted.* XENIA *goes into the house to talk to her mother.*

XENIA: Mum, I'm staying at Leah's tonight? Dad already said yes.

YOLANDA: Sit down and have something to eat.

XENIA: But we're not hungry, Mum, honest.

YOLANDA: Where's you brother? Nick! Come and have you dinner.

NICK: [*calling from the garage*] Mo is gonna be here in a minute, I just gotta do some things on the car before we go. We're gonna eat dinner later.

YOLANDA: Leah, please, sit down, eat something.

XENIA: Mum, we're right, okay. Leah doesn't eat.

YOLANDA: Leah, come on, you almost invisible.

XENIA: Mum.

YOLANDA: [*to herself*] You girls are too skinny. Stupid.

XENIA *goes out to* NICK.

XENIA: Hey, Nick? You still right for tonight?

NICK: Yeah, what doya reckon?

XENIA: We gotta be at Fox Studios by seven thirty, okay?

NICK: No worries.

XENIA: I told Mum we're going to the movies with you and Mo.

NICK: Yeah, but we're not going to the movies.

XENIA: Yeah, I know, but you gotta pick us up after.

NICK: No worries, sis. Hold that...

He gives her a spanner to hold. MOHAMMED *enters the house.*

MO: 'The Mo' has arrived. Howzitgoin', everyone?

YOLANDA: Hello, Mohammed.

MO: What's on the menu tonight, Mrs Nick's Mum? Smells great…

NICK: What are we seein'?

MO: … looks terrific…

XENIA: *Sound of Music 2*.

MO: … tastes superb.

NICK: I'm not watchin' that crap.

MO: Hey, Nick, we having dinner here before we go?

YOLANDA: You go tell him, Mo.

XENIA: Well whatever, okay?

NICK: Okay.

YOLANDA: [*calling*] Zubin! You want to eat? Is ready.

ZUBIN: [*from the garage*] Okay.

XENIA: Hey, Mo.

MO: Hey, Xenia.

> *They start to spar with each other.*

MO: Good day at school today?

XENIA: Yeah, we learnt all about bananas and plastic covers.

MO: Bananas and plastic covers. Hectic. Hey, Nick, what's happening, bro?

NICK: Just putting the new numberplate on the beast, man. I'll be with you in a minute and we'll make a move.

> XENIA *has gone into the room with* LEAH *to finish putting on her make-up.*

LEAH: Here, how do I look?

XENIA: Great. Oh my God, lippy.

LEAH: Don't put too much on, you don't want it smeared all over your face when your pashing off Will…

> LEAH *giggles with excitement.*

ZUBIN: [*looking at* NICK] Do you know what you are doing? That looks stupid. [*Now entering the dining room*] What's all this about bananas in pyjamas? We pay good money to send you to that school, not to learn about bananas. Come to the markets with me tomorrow if you want to see some bananas.

NICK: Okay, youse ready to go?

XENIA: Yeah. Dad, can I have some money for the movies please?

ZUBIN: How much?
XENIA: Twenty.
ZUBIN: What you gonna see?
XENIA: *Sound of Music 2.*
NICK: *Saw 9.*
XENIA: *Saw 9.*
NICK: *Sound of Music 2.*
XENIA: *Shrek 4.*

> *Small pause.*

ZUBIN: Movie marathon, eh? Well, be careful. And you, flip, [*to* NICK]
   be responsible.
NICK: No problemo.
XENIA: Right, we're ready.
YOLANDA: Xenia, what's all this stuff on your face? Just to see a film?
   Go back to your room and take it off.
XENIA: Mum. You're ruining my life.
NICK: Come on, we'll miss the movie, let's go, Mo.
YOLANDA: [*relenting*] Just go.
XENIA: Don't worry. I'll see you tomorrow.

> XENIA, NICK, MO *and* LEAH *leave.*

YOLANDA: We are too soft.
ZUBIN: Looks like we gonna be home alone tonight. Now do you want
   some cream on your pudding? Or do you want to eat some sausage
   first?

> *Music starts.*

SCENE FIVE: CLT.TZR

7.09 p.m. NICK *is driving his car with numberplate 'CLT.TZR'.* MO *is in
the passenger seat, with* LEAH *and* XENIA *in the back seat. The girls are
getting 'dressed up'.*

NICK: What are you two doing in the back?
LEAH: Changing.
NICK: Look, Leah, you can wear what you like, but listen, you, Xenia,
   you're not wearing that. Just stay in the clothes you're in. That skirt
   looks like a boob tube!

LEAH: Blow out, Nick.

NICK: Hey, you watch your mouth. I'm talking to my sister.

MO: Jesus, mate, you sound just like your mum.

NICK: Yeah, well she's my sister. You wear that and I'll tell Mum what you girls are really up to.

XENIA: Yeah, and I'll tell Dad that you guys went out and left us at the movies by ourselves.

NICK: Yeah? Well, go ahead and tell him. He'll kill me first and you later.

MO: He's just trying to be a good brother.

NICK: You look like lowie sluts.

XENIA: Get stuffed.

MO: I reckon they look good.

NICK: Shut up, Mo, you're supposed to back me up here, man.

MO: They should be able to wear what they like.

LEAH: That's right, you tell him, Mo?

MO: Hey, what are you girls up to anyway?

LEAH: Seein' a movie.

MO: Which one? Are you seeing *Apocalypse Again*... Hey, Nick, let's go see that.

NICK: What? You crazy? We got another agenda, man, you forgotten?

MO: Oh yeah. Well, what time do we have to pick youse up, ten thirty?

LEAH: Don't worry, we'll get a taxi.

MO: No, come on, we'll get yas at eleven, okay.

NICK: [*thinking it is too early and will wreck his night*] Eleven?

XENIA: Okay.

NICK: Bloody women.

LEAH: Okay! Just drop us here.

NICK: Just put your tights on under the skirt or something.

XENIA: Yeah, and you tuck your pants into your socks.

NICK: Don't smart-mouth me or it's a long walk home from Fox.

LEAH: See yas at eleven.

MO: Have a nice time.

> *The girls walk off.*

NICK: Good, now they're gone, let's head for the Oxford Tavern.

MO: Step on it, Mr Teezer.

> *The boys drive away.*

SCENE SIX: FOX STUDIOS

7.24 p.m. The girls are waiting outside Fox Studios.

XENIA: How do you know when it's them?

LEAH: He said it was a red Subaru Impreza WRX with 'TABOO' on the numberplate.

XENIA: Well, what if they don't come?

LEAH: They'll be here. Stop worrying.

> *Pause. A car drives past.*

XENIA: Is that them?

LEAH: That's a Lexus.

> *Another pause. Another car drives past.*

XENIA: What about that one?

LEAH: That's a Smart Car. Jesus, Xenia, get a grip.

> *Pause. Two* FILM BUFF KIDS *walk on dressed for the premiere of a new* Predator *movie. One has a* Predator *mask on and stands staring at the girls.*

FILM BUFF KID 2: There'll be all these quotes from the previous movies, you wait, someone'll say, [*quoting*] 'Billy, what's the matter?... We're all gonna die'... or what about that rasta guy from *Predator 2*, [*quoting*] 'Voodoo magic man', or [*saying this directly to* LEAH] 'Prepare yourself'.

LEAH: Get lost.

FILM BUFF KID 2: [*quoting again while dragging the* FILM BUFF KID 1 *away from the girls*] Get to the chopper, get to the chopper!

> *The* FILM BUFF KIDS *exit.*

LEAH: Year Seven newbies.

XENIA: What about that one?

LEAH: That's a Camry.

> *Pause.*

XENIA: They're not coming.

LEAH: Shut up.

> *Pause.*

XENIA: They're taking five hours. Let's go see *Predators Versus Heaps More Aliens*.

LEAH: Are we gonna have fun or are you gonna whinge all night…?

XENIA: Yeah but… you know… he's just a computer guy…

LEAH: Look, that's him… TABOO… It's him! [*She calls out and waves.*] Hi!

XENIA: Oh my God.

SCENE SEVEN: TABOO

7.38 p.m. iBoy *and* WILL *are in Will's car with 'TABOO' on the number-plate.*

iBoy: That's them. That's Leah. She looks better than on webcam.

> *They stop next to the girls.*

Hi. Leah?

LEAH: iBoy?

iBoy: Yeah. You girls want a ride?

LEAH: Sure.

> *The girls get in the back of the car.*

iBoy: This is Will.

LEAH: Hi. This is Xenia.

XENIA: Hi.

WILL: Hi.

iBoy: Wanna go straight to Will's place?

LEAH: Yeah, sure.

iBoy: Let's go.

> *Music starts and they drive.*

So we meet at last, eh?

LEAH: Yeah.

iBoy: Yeah. [*Small pause.*] Been waitin' long?

LEAH: No.

iBoy: Sweet. [*Another small uncomfortable pause.*] You two girls want something to drink? We'll stop off at a bottlo, eh?

LEAH: Yeah, sure.

iBoy: Any preferences?

LEAH: Oh, whatever. Diet Coke and Thins. Rum and Coke. Whatever.

iBOY: Like vodka?

LEAH: Yeah.

iBOY: Xenia?

Tiny embarrassed pause.

XENIA: Whatever.

iBOY: 'Whatever', it is.

He laughs, LEAH *laughs,* XENIA *smiles and squirms.* WILL *remains silent. Another small uncomfortable pause.*

There's a bottlo.

They stop at a bottle shop. WILL *gets out to buy the supplies.*

LEAH: Nice car.

iBOY: Yeah, cool, eh?!

LEAH: Yeah.

LEAH *looks at* XENIA *to say something.*

XENIA: Yeah, I love this car. Subaru WRX. And it's red, my favourite colour.

iBOY: Yeah, Will's a cool dude, I reckon, Xenia, you'll really like him. He's the guy online I was telling you about, Leah. You got a beautiful name.

LEAH: Thanks.

XENIA: He's quiet.

iBOY: Yeah, no, he lost his parents. That's why he's so quiet. He's funny as, when you get to know him. Smartest guy I know. He's the sort of mate you could ring and say I need a lift to Perth tomorrow and if he couldn't drive you there himself he'd give you his car no worries. He's a good mate to have. We've known each other for years.

LEAH: Right.

iBOY: S'pose you know everything about me already, Xenia?

XENIA: Not everything! Leah told me some stuff, but probably not everything.

WILL *returns with party supplies.*

WILL: Party supplies. Thins for you, Leah.

LEAH: Excellent. Thanks.

WILL: Mr Smirnoff.

iBoy: Excellent.

WILL: And I got you some Ferrero Rocher chocolates, Xenia.

XENIA: Great, thanks.

WILL: Let's go.

iBoy/LEAH: Yeah!

> *They drive away.*
>
> *Music builds.*

SONG: 'The Best Night of My Life'

> I am so excited, I am so delighted
> I can't get you off my mind.
> Come on baby,
> This will be the best night of my life
> This will be the best night of my life
> This will be the best night of my life
> This will be the best night of my life.

SCENE EIGHT: THE OXFORD TAVERN

8.05 p.m. NICK *and* MO *are at the Oxford Tavern, a well-known strippers pub. The music is pumping and there is a girl dancing around a pole.*

MC: That's right, fellas, this will be the best night of your life, welcome to the Oxford Tavern, where we've got hot and cold girls here all night. How 'bout a big hand for Chrystal!

NICK: This is it, Mo… the Oxford Tavern, best strip joint in Sydney.

MO: There's gotta be better joints than this, man, this is grungy as.

NICK: Whoa, look at the tits on her. Man, she is sex on legs…

MO: They're fake, man, implants, you can tell from here.

NICK: Who cares?

MO: I care. I want her to feel me when I'm touching them.

> *A voice comes over the microphone.*

MC: Okay, fellas, who wants to see Chrystal take it all off?

NICK: Woooooo, yeah!

MC: Come on, fellas, you're gonna have to make a lot more noise than that, come on, guys, let's hear it for Chrystal.

NICK: Come on, Chrystal, let's see ya without ya undies.

MO: I'm gonna go get a few beers, man, while it's still 'Happy Hour'.

NICK: Chrystal, Chrystal, Chrystal, yeah!

A reprise of the song comes up.

This will be the best night of my life
This will be the best night of my life
This will be the best night of my life
This will be the best night of my life.

The scene shifts.

SCENE NINE: THE DATE

8.26 p.m. iBOY, LEAH *and* XENIA *are in the lounge room in Will's apartment overlooking the beach.* WILL *is handing out the drinks.*

LEAH: Nice glasses. Crystal, eh?

iBOY: Yeah, there's heaps of nice things here, eh.

XENIA: Yeah, Leah told me you had a heated indoor pool.

WILL: Out the back.

XENIA: You must be really rich.

WILL: I work heaps for this I.T. company, plus I got left a bit from my parents.

LEAH: Yeah, sorry about your oldies. How'd they die?

XENIA: Leah?!

LEAH: I'm just asking.

WILL: Plane crash. On their second honeymoon.

LEAH: Oh, that's awful.

WILL: I was pretty young. I was real little actually. [*To* XENIA] Top up your drink?

XENIA: Yeah, alright.

iBOY: [*to* LEAH] Sorry I can't impress you with an Impreza. Did you bring your swimmers?

LEAH: Nar.

iBOY: Bummer.

LEAH: Not necessarily.

XENIA: Must be good watching all the surfies through this telescope. I bet you look at chicks through it too?

WILL: Mostly the stars.

XENIA: I'm right into astrology too.

WILL: Cool. What star sign are you?

XENIA: Arrh… Aquarius.

WILL: Aquarius. What day?

XENIA: Third of February.

WILL: Cool.

XENIA: What star sign are you?

WILL: Scorpio.

XENIA: Cool.

iBoy: Hey, I'll show you Will's studio. [*Calling to* WILL] Hey, Will, is it cool if we check out the studio?

WILL: Yeah.

> iBoy *takes* LEAH *into the studio.* XENIA *and* WILL *drift back into the lounge room.*

XENIA: Leah said you're twenty.

WILL: Is that what she said?

XENIA: Yeah. But how how old are you really?

WILL: How old are you?

XENIA: I asked first.

WILL: I asked second.

XENIA: Yeah, but I asked first.

WILL: Yeah, but who asks first has to answer first.

XENIA: [*with embarrassed laughter*] No, that's not how it works…

> *They both laugh, enjoying each other's company.*

WILL: I'm twenty-eight.

XENIA: Twenty-eight. [*Now not laughing*] Oh my God.

LEAH: Hey, Leah, check out all the guitars…

iBoy: Yeah…

> *The music comes up and they play 'Will's Studio Jam'. The scene shifts.*

SCENE TEN: THE OXFORD TAVERN

9.50 p.m. NICK *and* MO *are still at the Oxford Tavern.*

MC: And that was the the lovely Delilah, what about the jugs on her, eh, fellas!

NICK: Yeah, wooooo!

MO: She's a good dancer, eh, how come she's working here? She should be in the Australian Ballet or something.

NICK: 'Cause she's a slut and she loves it.

MC: Don't forget, fellas, Gladys is coming around with the meat raffle, so dig deep, first prize is a leg of lamb.

MO: Meat raffle, now we're talking. [*Looking at his watch*] Maybe we should go soon, pick up you sister, eh.

NICK: Nar, we got ages. Not even ten yet.

MC: Okay, fellas, hang around, Madison will be out in just a few minutes, we got girls all night tonight, fellas, so grab yourselves another drink.

NICK: Madison! She's the chick who came out with the maid outfit before... Sex on Legs. Whoa, man, she was hot—I'm not going till I see her again. She'll have a school uniform on for sure, one of those short tartan skirts... She does the blow job on stage, mate, don't you wanna stick around for a blow job?

MO: I don't want a blow job, man, I want a leg of lamb.

NICK: [*noticing a girl on the other side of the room*] Hey, did you see the way that chick looked at me?

MO: Who?

NICK: That chick over there, look at her.

MO: The prostitute?

NICK: Yeah, I mean no, I mean I'm just gonna go over and say 'g'day'.

MO: Don't go near her, man, that's what she wants.

NICK: I'll just say 'g'day' and we'll make a move...

> NICK *leaves.*

MC: Here she is, fellas, the one you've all been waiting for, the one, the only, Madison...

MO: [*at Madison*] Show us your Square Garden, baby! [*Looking for* NICK] Hey, Nick? Nick!

> *He goes off looking for* NICK *as the music swells again and the scene shifts.*

SCENE ELEVEN: THE RAPE

9.51 p.m. Back at Will's place, a few drinks into the evening, the girls are dancing.

LEAH: Hey, let's watch a movie on the plasma... Will's got *Ocean's Fourteen*, eh, seen that? I love Matt Clooney.

The others howl with laughter at LEAH.

What?

XENIA: God, my head is spinning a bit. Where's your bathroom?

WILL: Just down the hall to the left. I'll show ya.

LEAH *looks through the DVD stack, pulls out one and puts it on.*

LEAH: Oh, you've got *Love Actually 2*, I love this movie, it's full of love, and like all this love and everyone loves each other, like, except one guy who hates everyone, he's great, he's really funny.

iBoy: Yeah, Will's got a great collection, eh. Seen that one?

iBoy *points at a member of the audience like he/she's a DVD on the rack.* LEAH *looks at the audience like they are a movie title.*

LEAH: Errrrr, no way, I hate that one, *The Zombie Returns Again*, no, yuck, no way... Oh, what about the periscope, show me the periscope...

iBoy: Telescope.

LEAH: Whatever whatever whatever... periscope, telescope...

Meanwhile, XENIA *has gone to the bathroom. The alcohol is making her sick. She splashes water on her face and steadies herself on the rim of the sink and looks at her reflection in the mirror.*

WILL: You okay?

XENIA: Yeah.

LEAH: Let me see, let me see... [*She bangs her eye on the telescope.*] Oh, my eye. That really hurt, I've never been in so much pain in my whole life as now, owww.

XENIA *comes out of the bathroom.*

iBoy: We'll go to the fridge and get something for your eye.

WILL *leads* XENIA *into a bedroom, closes the door behind him and sits her on the bed.*

LEAH: Yeah, ouch, my eye...

iBoy: That's why they call me 'iBoy'.

LEAH: [*laughing*] You are just, like, the funniest, like, you know, guy, in the world, ever.

He gets her a cold bottle of Coke and she rests it on her eye.

WILL *starts to caress* XENIA, *she becomes uncomfortable.*

iBOY: [*to* LEAH] You want to see a good trick?

LEAH: Yeah.

WILL *goes to kiss* XENIA *but she backs away.*

XENIA: No…

iBOY: Pass me that packet of Mentos.

XENIA: [*getting off the bed*] I don't think I should be doing this.

WILL: It's alright.

WILL *takes her hand and sits* XENIA *back on the bed.*

iBOY: You'll love this.

XENIA: I don't want to be here.

iBOY: So I take this Mentos, and I put it in this bottle of Coke.

WILL *then reaches up under* XENIA*'s skirt and starts pulling off her tights.*

LEAH: What the hell are you doing, this is crazy.

XENIA: What are you doing?

iBOY: You'll see.

XENIA: Don't… stop it.

WILL: It's alright. Shhh.

He puts his hand over her mouth.

iBOY: Okay… you ready…

XENIA *tries to get up but* WILL *pushes her down again. He then spreads her legs, undoes his belt, and they freeze.*

iBOY *shakes up the Coke bottle with the Mentos in it and there is an almighty explosion.*

LEAH: Oh my God, that's incredible, that is so amazing. That's the funniest thing I've ever seen in my whole life. Wait, do it again, I'll take a picture of it and it'll be on my phone… Do it again, where's my phone…? Phone, phone, come on, little phoney, where are you…?

iBOY: I'll be right back.

LEAH *looks for her phone while* iBOY *goes down the hall to the bedroom. He goes in, just as* WILL *is doing his pants up. They look at each other.* XENIA *is covering her face.*

WILL: Your turn.

> WILL *leaves, closes the door behind him and goes back to the kitchen to pour himself another drink.*

> iBoy *undoes his belt and walks towards* XENIA.

> WILL *joins* LEAH *in the lounge room.*

XENIA: No, get away…

LEAH: You seen my phone?

> As iBoy *tries to get on top of* XENIA *she kicks at him.*

WILL: You want another drink?

iBoy: You want me to smash this bottle on your face? Eh? You want me to cut you up?

LEAH: Yeah sure… Xenia, where's my phone?

> LEAH *heads for the bedroom.*

WILL: Leah?

> LEAH *stops and turns back to* WILL.

iBoy: You say something and I'll cut your throat?

WILL: Hey, you seen *Sex and the City Part 2*?

LEAH: No, put it on. I've always wanted to see that.

WILL: It's got a great ending.

> iBoy *pushes* XENIA *back down, opens her arms out, and freezes.*

> WILL *puts on the DVD, and they sit together and watch it, eating chips.*

LEAH: How long you known iBoy?

WILL: Few years.

LEAH: What's his real name 'cause he won't tell me?

WILL: I don't know.

LEAH: Yes you do, come on, what is it?

WILL: I can't tell you, it's a secret.

LEAH: Yeah, as if.

WILL: That's classified information.

> *Without saying a word,* iBoy *leaves the room and goes back to the lounge room with the others.*

iBoy: What youse watchin?

LEAH: Hey, is your real name 'Classified Information'?

iBOY: What?

LEAH: He, Will, your friend, said your name is, what was it again?

iBOY: Want another drink?

LEAH: Sure, where's Xenia?

iBOY: Out with the telescope, she's so into the stars I was getting bored.

WILL: Yeah.

LEAH: Yeah, she can be a bit of a nerd. Hey, Xenia, where are ya? Come and have another drink.

WILL: Yeah, good idea.

> LEAH *laughs hysterically. Meanwhile,* XENIA *has pulled her tights back on and has come back into the lounge room.*

LEAH: God, Xenia, you look like your spinning out. Come and sit down, we're watching, what is it again, oh look… oh, yeah…

> LEAH *starts to do an impersonation of the 'Stop Video Piracy' advertisement on the DVD.*

'Would you steal a mobile phone?' Yeah… 'Would you steal a movie?' Yeah… 'Stop video piracy…' Yeah, I download heaps of movies…

> XENIA *watches. They all watch for a while eating chips.*

> *The tension is unbearable.*

> *Long pause, only the sound of munching and the movie.*

XENIA: Let's go.

LEAH: No, we still got some time, eh, it's still only ten or something. Let's stay a bit longer. We're watching the movie. After the movie.

XENIA: Nick will be waiting outside Fox, come on.

LEAH: No they won't.

XENIA: Please, I wanna go.

LEAH: [*unimpressed*] Ohhh.

iBOY: Na, Leah, we can all catch each other another night. I think we better take yas back.

XENIA: No, Leah… Let's get a cab.

LEAH: God, Xenia… I want to stay.

> *A very ugly pause.*

Alright then but we're getting a lift with these guys, okay?

XENIA: No, I'll call a taxi.

WILL: No you won't. We'll give you a lift back. I'll bring the car around.

iBoy: No problem. We'll drop you girls back at Fox. Okay?

LEAH: [*still unimpressed*] Okay. [*To* XENIA] Okay?

XENIA: [*hiding her agony*] Okay.

> *The scene shifts.*

SCENE TWELVE: TABOO

10.39 p.m. Back in 'TABOO'. Now LEAH *is sitting in the back seat with* iBoy. XENIA *is sitting very uncomfortably in the front.*

iBoy: You okay, Xenia? You look like you're spinning out a bit?

LEAH: You tell the guys if you want to stop, Xenia, you don't want to spew all over Will's car. Hey, thanks for a great night, what are you guys doing next Friday?

iBoy: Catching up with you two I hope.

LEAH: Yeah, for sure. [*She turns to* XENIA.] Maybe drink a bit less next time.

> *There is a long silence until they arrive at Fox Studios.*

WILL: Here we are, Fox Studios.

> *The two girls get out of the car.*

LEAH: [*to* iBoy] Hey, get on Facebook when you get home later.

iBoy: Yeah, for sure. Hey, Leah, come here.

> *She leans in the window and he whispers to her.*

I think I might be falling in love. See ya.

> *He kisses her. She smiles.*

LEAH: See yas.

> *The girls leave. Small pause.*

> iBoy *looks at* WILL.

iBoy: Plane crash on their second honeymoon?

> *They both howl with laughter and then drive off.*

SCENE THIRTEEN: FOX STUDIOS

10.55 p.m. XENIA *runs to the nearest bush and vomits.*

LEAH: God, Xenia, you really did drink too much. You okay? You look like you're in pain. You are so pissed. Dad won't be too impressed when we get home. Just tell him you got your period. Where's this stupid mongrel brother of yours? We could of stayed there longer.

> XENIA*'s phone rings.*

Aren't you going to answer that? It might be your brother.

> XENIA *answers the phone.*

WILL: [*voice*] If you tell anyone what happened, we're gonna kill you. You got that... we're gonna...

> XENIA *hangs up and stands in shock.*

LEAH: Was that your brother?

XENIA: No... wrong number. Where the hell is he?!

LEAH: Relax, he'll be here. God, what is with you?

> *The two* FILM BUFF KIDS *re-enter, as if the film has ended and they are leaving Fox Studios.*

FILM BUFF KID 2: See, I told you, the Predator always wins! How about that kid same kid from P2, now all grown up: 'Want some candy?' Yeah, but how cool was the half Alien-half Predator? ... when she takes his helmet off and she says, 'You are one ugly motherf...' and right at the end he looked at her and he said... [*Looking at* XENIA] 'Shit happens'... hahahahahahah...

> *They both laugh louder and exit.*

LEAH: Losers.

> *Pause.*

XENIA: Leah?

LEAH: What? [*Pause.*] What is it? Yeah, I know, you're sorry you stuffed up my night. Get over it.

> *Pause.* XENIA *sees* NICK*'s car and runs out onto the road.*

XENIA: Here, we're over here!

LEAH: They can see you, just calm down.

> NICK *and* MO *pull up.*

SCENE FOURTEEN: CLT.TZR

11.01 p.m.

MO: Good evening, girls? How was *The Sound of Music 2*?

NICK: Jesus, Xenia, you look like shit, what's wrong? Hey, you stink of spew and alcohol. You two have been drinking, haven't you?

LEAH: No.

NICK: Yes you have, I can smell it. You are so lucky we're taking you to Leah's. Mum and Dad would kill you. Are you crazy pissing on at your age.

LEAH: Get off our backs, will you, and just drive.

MO: You girls want some Mentos to hide the smell from your dad?

LEAH: Yeah, thanks, Mo.

NICK: You know what, Leah, the worst thing my sister ever did was hang around with you.

LEAH: Shut your face.

NICK: I wish she never met you.

LEAH: And I wish I had never met you.

MO: Hey, come on, you two, take it easy. Come on, bro, we had a few drinks at their age.

NICK: Yeah, well they're girls, and she's my sister.

MO: It's like you're racist against women, man. Like, I believe that this whole world is racist against women.

NICK: Just shut up why don't you, Mo.

MO: Sorry to upset you, mate.

NICK: I'm fine. Just don't do it again, Xenia.

XENIA: Stop the car.

> *She opens the door and vomits again.*

NICK: Youse have mixed your drinks with ecstacy, haven't yas?

LEAH: No, she's just tired.

NICK: You sure you don't want to just come home?

XENIA: Go to Leah's.

NICK: Okay, just don't do it again.

LEAH: Can you just drive us home, Mr Self-Righteous?

MO: You okay?

XENIA: Yeah, I'm fine.

> XENIA*'s phone rings again.*

NICK: Now what? Who's trying to ring you at this time of night?
LEAH: Aren't you going to answer it?

The phone keeps ringing, XENIA *not wanting to answer it.*

NICK: Answer it. Answer it.

The phone keeps ringing as the scene shifts.

SCENE FIFTEEN: LEAH'S HOME

11.19 p.m. LEAH *and* XENIA *enter Leah's home.* CHAD *is still on computer.*

LEAH: Hi, Dad.
CHAD: How was the movie?
LEAH: Oh, pretty boring.
CHAD: What did you think, Xenia?

She doesn't answer.

LEAH: I think she ate too much crap, she's feeling a bit sick. [*Unimpressed with* XENIA] I'm gonna take my make-up off.

LEAH *leaves.* XENIA *hesitates. Long pause.*

CHAD: What's going on, you two have a fight?

LEAH *comes out of the bathroom.*

LEAH: Your turn.

LEAH *goes into her room and sits on the bed and starts texting* iBoy. XENIA*'s phone rings. She ignores it.* XENIA *turns her phone off.*

Long pause.

CHAD: Too many Twisties, eh?

XENIA *slowly walks into Leah's bedroom. She stands looking at* LEAH.

LEAH: So did you have sex with Will or what? Or did you chicken out at the last minute? That's why you wanted to leave, wasn't it? I thought you were my friend, Xenia. I should go on my own next time.
XENIA: They raped me.
LEAH: Yeah, right.
XENIA: Both of them. Both of them did… while you were in the next room.

XENIA *holds back the tears trying to contain herself.*

LEAH: You had sex with my boyfriend?

XENIA: They both raped me, Leah… I didn't want to… they made me…

> *Pause.*

LEAH: Do you wanna go home?

XENIA: I…

> XENIA *is not sure what to do.*

LEAH: We'll tell my dad you're sick… if you wanna go home…

> *Pause. No answer from* XENIA. LEAH *gets off the bed and goes to leave the room. She still doesn't quite believe* XENIA.

XENIA: Leah…

LEAH: What? I'm just gonna get Dad to drive you home.

XENIA: Don't you believe me?

LEAH: Yeah. [*Pause. She starts to believe* XENIA.] Yeah, okay, I believe you…

> *Pause. She comforts* XENIA.

I believe you. [*She starts to feel ashamed of her reaction.*] I'm sorry. [*Another small pause.*] What do you want to do?

XENIA: I don't know.

> LEAH *decides for her. She leaves the room and goes to her father.* XENIA *stands alarmed.*

LEAH: Dad?

CHAD: Yeah?

LEAH: Xenia's not feeling very well, can you drive her home?

CHAD: What sort of 'not feeling very well'? If youse have had a fight, then work it out please, I'm not being a taxi driver at this time of night. It's eleven thirty or something.

> *Small pause as* LEAH *thinks what to say.* XENIA *comes into the room.* LEAH *moves closer to her dad.*

LEAH: No, honestly, she's feeling real sick. Aren't ya, Xenia?

CHAD: You girls stink of grog and smoke, where have youse been?

LEAH: The movies, I told ya.

CHAD: I can smell it on your breath Leah. Xenia?

LEAH: We went to the pictures, Dad, God. Why the big interrogation all of a sudden? Don't you trust me or what? We went to the movies, that's all, that's the truth. If it's too late for you to drive Xenia home... then we'll call a cab.

CHAD: Alright then... I'll drive her home.

The scene shifts.

SCENE SIXTEEN: XENIA'S HOUSE

11.55 p.m. Xenia's house.

ZUBIN *stands at the front door in his dressing-gown.* CHAD *and* LEAH *are at the door having just brought* XENIA *home.* XENIA *waits just inside the door behind her father.*

CHAD: Well, sorry about the late hour... but I thought it would be best to bring her home the way she was feeling...

ZUBIN: Yes.

CHAD: You feeling bit better now, Xenia?

XENIA nods.

ZUBIN: Thank you for bringing her home.

Very uncomfortable pause. CHAD *nods.*

CHAD: [*trying to calm* ZUBIN *down*] Yeah, well, at this age, eh...

He leans in to quietly tell ZUBIN *something so the girls won't hear.*

Look... I reckon they went somewhere, had a few drinks, maybe a cigarette or two and your girl got a bit sick, you know, that's all, she'll be right.

ZUBIN: And you think this is okay your daughter going drinking and smoking at her age? Taking my girl with her. Teaching her these things?

XENIA: Dad.

CHAD: I'm not saying I approve...

ZUBIN: Dressed like that. Like some girl on the street.

CHAD: Now wait just a minute, mate...

ZUBIN: Is no wonder my girl is sick.

XENIA: Dad.

ZUBIN: Thank you for bringing my daughter home. You won't have to do that again.

An ugly uncomfortable pause.

LEAH: Come on, Dad. See ya tomorrow, Xenia.

CHAD *doesn't pursue the argument. They exit.*

ZUBIN *then turns in and looks at* XENIA. XENIA *is a mess.*

YOLANDA *enters.*

ZUBIN: Where did you go tonight? Not to the movies, eh? Where? Tell me. And don't lie to me. You meet some boys, you get drunk, what else?

YOLANDA: That's enough.

ZUBIN: Is not enough. You let her go out and wear these clothes and all that make-up, this is all your fault. You are the foolish one in the first place and now look what happened.

XENIA: Please, don't shout.

ZUBIN: It is no use to cry, now tell me the truth.

XENIA: We went out with these two guys.

Pause. XENIA *looks at her mother, starts to cry.*

ZUBIN: Which boys, who?

Tense pause.

XENIA: They raped me.

Both parents are shocked. This was unexpected. Long pause.

ZUBIN: Where's your brother? Nickola?

XENIA: Please, don't shout.

ZUBIN: Nickola? Nick!

NICK: What! Jesus.

ZUBIN: Look at your sister. Come and look what you done, you stupid boy.

NICK: What, I didn't do nothin'.

ZUBIN: Where did youse go?

NICK: We took them to the pictures like they wanted.

YOLANDA: Don't lie to us.

NICK: I'm not lying.

ZUBIN: Tell us the truth.

NICK: I am telling you the truth. [*Pause. He sees* XENIA'*s state.*] What happened?

ZUBIN: I told you to be responsible for your sister. This is all your fault.

NICK: Bullshit.

> YOLANDA *slaps* NICK *in the face. He stands stunned. He then leaves. Pause.*

ZUBIN: Who are these boys? What are their names? I want to know their names. Where do they live? Tell me. I'll kill the bastards.

XENIA: I don't know their names. I don't know where they live. They probably lied about everything. Everything's all a lie. They keep calling me saying they'll kill me if I tell anyone, but I don't know what to tell, I don't want to answer any questions about it, I just want to be left alone. I just want… to be left alone.

> *Very ugly pause.*

> XENIA *goes to her room while* ZUBIN *and* YOLANDA *stand in the lounge stunned and confused about what to do or say.*

YOLANDA: We must go to the police.

ZUBIN: The police here will not help us. No-one will help us. They all gonna say she deserve it. I don't want that. I don't trust them.

> *Pause.* YOLANDA *goes to Xenia's room very slowly.*

YOLANDA: Xenia? Xenia?

> *She enters.* ZUBIN *slowly walks over to the doorway of her room and looks in.* XENIA *looks up at them.* YOLANDA *sits next to her and puts her arm around her. They hug.*

> ZUBIN *starts to cry.*

> *Pause.* YOLANDA *is cradling* XENIA, *then wipes away her tears.*

> *Pause.*

> XENIA *stands.* YOLANDA *stands too.*

XENIA: I want to go to the police.

> ZUBIN *nods his head in agreement.*

> *Pause.*

> *The lights fade to blackout.*

Lights up as music starts for the final song.

SONG: 'Tegan'

> The way she spoke
> The way she dressed
> The way she seemed on the outside
> Thousands of questions
> Millions like her
> But she had the courage to face them on trial.

> Too many unseen, too many unheard
> Too many spiders free to invade
> Her name doesn't matter, her shame didn't fester
> Her actions spoke louder than words.

> In just one day
> My life has changed
> I'm no longer the girl I wanted to be
> I'll find the strength
> I'll take the stand
> And I'll have the courage to face them on trial.

> Too many unseen, too many unheard
> Too many spiders free to invade
> Tegan Wagner, her shame didn't fester
> Her actions spoke louder than words.

THE END